Vegetable Garden Handbook

A PLANNING & PLANTING RECORD BOOK

by Roger Griffith

illustrations by Cathy Baker

Published in the United States by Garden Way Publishing, Charlotte, Vermont 05445. Printed by the George Little Press.

Second Revised Printing, April 1975

International Standard Book Number: 0-88266-028-4

Welcome to Better Gardening

This Vegetable Garden Handbook is designed to help you, the serious gardener, whether you are a beginner or more experienced.

Here is the information you need to guide you in raising most of the vegetable crops raised in this country.

Here, too, are other valuable helps. Garden plans for three years—these are useful in planting and for proper crop rotation plans. And space to record information about all of your crops—when you planted and harvested them, and whether you liked them. There's space, too, for annual cost records, weather summaries and much more.

To get the most out of this book, you must do your part. Find out from the Extension Service, fellow gardeners or a garden supply house the average dates of the last spring frost and of the first fall frost in your immediate area and record them here:

Last Spring Frost   First Fall Frost

You'll need this information in planning what you should plant, and when.

In deciding what crops you will raise, consider several things: The length of the growing season in your area, the suitability of your garden soil for various crops, and, most important, the eating habits of your family. A 50-foot row of broccoli may look beautiful in your garden, but it may make your family swear off broccoli for life.

Experiment with varieties, keeping a record in this book of those experiments, and your opinion of the results. Try something new each year.

Keep a careful record this year, and see how valuable it is in your planning next year.

*Varieties marked *are recommended for freezing.*

Good Gardening!

Select a scale that fits your garden plan. Scale of 1 inch=10 feet can be used for garden 70 by 50 feet or smaller. Scale of 1 inch=5 feet for garden 35 by 25½ feet or smaller. Each square here measures a half-inch.

19__________Garden Plan

YEAR'S GARDENING, 19______

Last spring frost ______ First fall frost ______

Notes on season's weather ______

Problems, achievements ______

YEAR'S EXPENSES

Items	Cost	Items	Cost
Seeds		Tools, Supplies	
Plants			
Fertilizer, Mulch		Other expenses	
Total		Total	

TOTAL for year ______

Select a scale that fits your garden plan. Scale of 1 inch=10 feet can be used for garden 70 by 50 feet or smaller. Scale of 1 inch=5 feet for garden 35 by 25½ feet or smaller. Each square here measures a half-inch.

19__________Garden Plan

YEAR'S GARDENING, 19________

________________________ Last spring frost

________________________ First fall frost

Notes on season's weather________________________

____

____

Problems, achievements ________________________

____

____

YEAR'S EXPENSES

Items	Cost
Seeds ________	________
________	________
________	________
________	________
________	________
Plants ________	________
________	________
________	________
________	________
________	________
________	________
Fertilizer, Mulch	
________	________
________	________
________	________
________	________
________	________
________	________
________	________
Total	________

Items	Cost
Tools, Supplies ________	________
________	________
________	________
________	________
________	________
________	________
________	________
________	________
________	________
________	________
________	________
________	________
________	________
Other expenses	
________	________
________	________
________	________
________	________
________	________
Total	________

TOTAL for year ________________________

Select a scale that fits your garden plan. Scale of 1 inch=10 feet can be used for garden 70 by 50 feet or smaller. Scale of 1 inch=5 feet for garden 35 by 25½ feet or smaller. Each square here measures a half-inch.

19__________Garden Plan

YEAR'S GARDENING, 19________

________________________ ________________________
Last spring frost First fall frost

Notes on season's weather________________________
____
____

Problems, achievements ________________________
____
____

YEAR'S EXPENSES

Items	Cost	Items	Cost
Seeds ________	____	Tools, Supplies ____	____
________	____	________	____
________	____	________	____
________	____	________	____
________	____	________	____
Plants ________	____	________	____
________	____	________	____
________	____	________	____
________	____	________	____
________	____	________	____
________	____	________	____
Fertilizer, Mulch		________	____
________	____	________	____
________	____	Other expenses	
________	____	________	____
________	____	________	____
________	____	________	____
________	____	________	____
________	____	________	____
Total	____	Total	____

TOTAL for year ________________________

ARTICHOKE, JERUSALEM *(Helianthus tuberosus)* Perennial tuber of sunflower family. American origin and once cultivated by Indians. Contains no starch, stores sugar as levulose, so is good for diabetics. Low in calories. Free from disease and pests. So prolific it will spread through garden unless checked. Grows throughout the United States. Two quarts of roots needed for 25-foot row.

PLANTING: Plant in location where their 6-8 foot growth will not shade other vegetables. Plant in fall, or in spring as early as soil can be worked, placing whole tubers, or chunky sections, four inches deep, two feet apart in rows three to four feet apart. Growing season of 125 days.

HARVESTING: After frost, cut tops back. Tubers can be dug then, or at any time until spring. Since they do not store well, they should be dug when needed. Can be stored for up to month if kept moist. This is a good experimental crop. It is not related to, nor does it look or taste like green or globe artichokes. Can be boiled or mashed (good with a taste of nutmeg added), cooked in cream sauce, broiled, fried or added raw to salad after being skinned and cut into small pieces.

VARIETY: *American* is recommended. It is smooth-surfaced, size of man's fist and not knobby.

19 VARIETY	DATE PLANTED	AMOUNT PLANTED (ROW LENGTH)
1.		
2.		
3.		

HARVEST DATES VARIETY	EXPECTED	ACTUAL
1.		
2.		
3.		

SATISFIED WITH VARIETY, AMOUNT?

1.
2.
3.

NOTES

19 VARIETY	DATE PLANTED	AMOUNT PLANTED (ROW LENGTH)
1.		
2.		
3.		

HARVEST DATES VARIETY	EXPECTED	ACTUAL
1.		
2.		
3.		

SATISFIED WITH VARIETY, AMOUNT?

1.
2.
3.

NOTES

19 VARIETY	DATE PLANTED	AMOUNT PLANTED (ROW LENGTH)
1.		
2.		
3.		

HARVEST DATES VARIETY	EXPECTED	ACTUAL
1.		
2.		
3.		

SATISFIED WITH VARIETY, AMOUNT?

1.
2.
3.

NOTES

ASPARAGUS *(Asparagus officinalis)* Perennial. An asparagus bed is a must for the gourmet gardener. Grows well throughout United States as far south as southern Georgia. Thirty-five roots in 50-foot row will yield about 15 pounds, half of what an asparagus-loving family will require for meals, canning and freezing.

PLANTING: Only the patient gardener will plant asparagus seeds and wait two years for the first taste of this delicious vegetable, and that gardener has the time to look elsewhere for instructions. Select garden site in section where bed will not interfere with annual crops. In spring, when soil can be worked, dig trench 12-14 inches deep, 10 inches wide. In bottom of trench dig in six-inch layer of compost and rotted manure, plus lime if needed to maintain neutral pH. Set year-old or two-year-old roots 18 inches apart, cover with two inches of soil. As shoots appear, add soil gradually, so that during summer, trench is filled. This filling must be done slowly to avoid stifling plants. If more than one row is planned, set them four feet apart. This space is needed for the tremendous root system that will develop. Asparagus planted in a 12-inch to 18-inch wide bed will provide a hedge in summer.

CULTIVATION: Protect bed each winter with heavy mulch of straw or hay. This should be pulled away in spring to speed up the warming of the soil. Continued mulching reduces cultivation required. Each fall add blanket of manure or compost. Asparagus is heavy feeder.

HARVESTING: Resist temptation to sample the first year, and keep cutting season short the second year. In the following years, cutting can begin when shoots reach 4-8 inches tall and before scales on tips begin to open. Pick by breaking the shoots by hand just below surface of soil. Halt harvesting when shoots become too thin (less than half-inch in diameter), about July 1, and permit shoots to grow remainder of season, reaching 5-10 feet in height.

ENEMIES: Several beetles are attracted to asparagus and should be sought out and picked early in the morning. Poultry allowed to ramble in bed will do the job, too. Asparagus rust can be avoided with rust-resistant varieties.

VARIETIES: In early part of century, rust threatened entire commercial crop, and resulted in an intensive development program. The result was **Mary Washington* (Most widely grown, good fresh, canned or frozen), **Martha Washington* and, later, **Viking* (or *Mary Washington Improved,* widely grown in the Midwest) all rust-resistant.

19	VARIETY	DATE PLANTED	AMOUNT PLANTED (ROW LENGTH)
1.			
2.			
3.			

HARVEST DATES	VARIETY	EXPECTED	ACTUAL
1.			
2.			
3.			

SATISFIED WITH VARIETY, AMOUNT?

1. ______
2. ______
3. ______

NOTES ______

19	VARIETY	DATE PLANTED	AMOUNT PLANTED (ROW LENGTH)
1.			
2.			
3.			

HARVEST DATES	VARIETY	EXPECTED	ACTUAL
1.			
2.			
3.			

SATISFIED WITH VARIETY, AMOUNT?

1. ______
2. ______
3. ______

NOTES ______

19	VARIETY	DATE PLANTED	AMOUNT PLANTED (ROW LENGTH)
1.			
2.			
3.			

HARVEST DATES	VARIETY	EXPECTED	ACTUAL
1.			
2.			
3.			

SATISFIED WITH VARIETY, AMOUNT?

1. ______
2. ______
3. ______

NOTES ______

BEANS, BUSH, YELLOW AND GREEN *(Phaseolus vulgaris)* Easy to grow, productive, can be grown throughout the United States and will do well in almost any soil. Because they are a quick crop, beans can be interplanted with cabbage and harvested before cabbage needs space. Grow 15-20 inches tall. Beans planted near potatoes will help latter by repelling the Colorado potato beetle. Four ounces of seed in a 50-foot row will yield 25 pounds of beans.

PLANTING: Dust seeds with nitrogen inoculant to build nitrogen into soil and increase yield. About date of last frost, sow seed 2-4 inches apart, covering with 1-1½ inches of soil, in rows 18-24 inches apart. Thin to 4-6 inches apart. Avoid large plantings, with too many beans for family use, unless they are wanted for freezing or canning. Instead, a succession of plantings every two weeks, until 7-8 weeks before first fall frost, will provide a continuing supply. Seeds germinate in 4-7 days, but will rot if planted in cold, wet soil.

CULTIVATION: Avoid cultivation after rain or when dew is on plants, since working in plants when they are wet may spread diseases. Beans are shallow rooted, so hoe gently. Add mulch, but only after plants are up and soil is warm.

HARVESTING: Stay away when plants are damp. Pick early and often, when pods are nearly full grown, but beans are not fully developed and pods are still crisp. If development has progressed too far, delay picking, then pick beans for use as shell or dry beans.

ENEMIES: The Mexican bean beetle, tan with eight black spots on each wing, is larger than a ladybug. Search for, pick and destroy beetles, to prevent them from laying egg clusters on undersides of leaves. It is larvae from these eggs that ravage leaves, then eat beans. During harvesting, watch for egg clusters and destroy them. Interplant with clumps of nasturtiums, garlic. Rotenone also used for beetle control. Fungus diseases are carried in the seed, spread by gardeners when plants are wet. Burn diseased vines. Select seeds resistant to some of these ills, such as the rusts. If young bean plants are found eaten on the ground, suspect your neighborhood woodchucks. Cutworms may cut young plants at ground level. Scatter wood ashes in the row, then soak them.

VARIETIES: Green include: **Improved Tendergreen* (56 days to harvest. Meaty, dark green, stringless, mosaic resistant). **Tendercrop* (53 days. Smooth round green pods, mosaic resistant). Yellow varieties are **Brittle Wax* (52 days. Heavy yields). *Pencil Pod Wax* (54 days. Hardy, heavy yielder, good for late fall or early spring plantings).

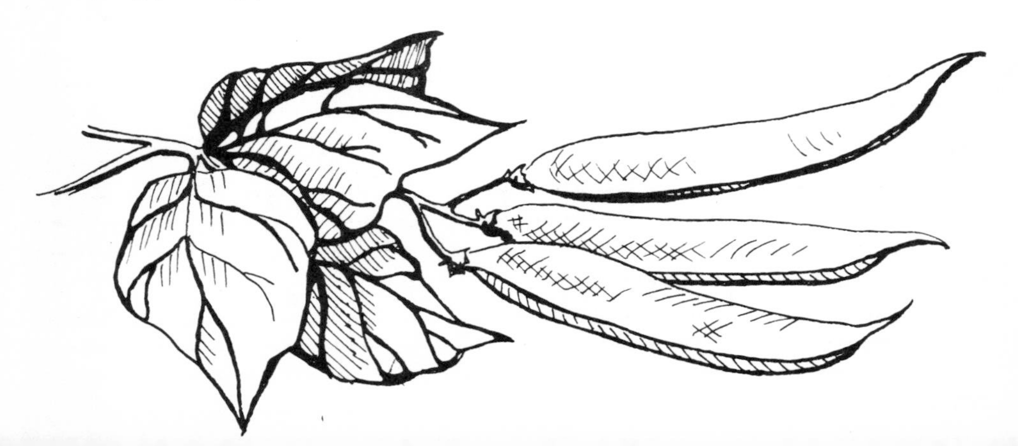

19	VARIETY	DATE PLANTED	AMOUNT PLANTED (ROW LENGTH)
1.			
2.			
3.			

HARVEST DATES	VARIETY	EXPECTED	ACTUAL
1.			
2.			
3.			

SATISFIED WITH VARIETY, AMOUNT?

1.			
2.			
3.			

NOTES

19	VARIETY	DATE PLANTED	AMOUNT PLANTED (ROW LENGTH)
1.			
2.			
3.			

HARVEST DATES	VARIETY	EXPECTED	ACTUAL
1.			
2.			
3.			

SATISFIED WITH VARIETY, AMOUNT?

1.			
2.			
3.			

NOTES

19	VARIETY	DATE PLANTED	AMOUNT PLANTED (ROW LENGTH)
1.			
2.			
3.			

HARVEST DATES	VARIETY	EXPECTED	ACTUAL
1.			
2.			
3.			

SATISFIED WITH VARIETY, AMOUNT?

1.			
2.			
3.			

NOTES

BEANS, BUSH, SHELL *(Phaseolus vulgaris)* Grown for shelling from pods, then eaten green, or dried before use. Dozens of types, many native to the United States and dating back to its earliest history. These and other types are doubly valuable to the gardener since they enrich the garden soil with nitrogen. These beans and all others are good to plant where some "hungry" crop, such as corn, grew previous year. Four ounces of seed for 50-foot row will yield eight pounds shelled.

PLANTING: Dust seed with nitrogen inoculant. When soil is warm, danger of spring frosts is past, sow seed 2-4 inches apart, cover with 1-1½ inches of light soil. Thin plants to 4-6 inches apart. Space rows 18-24 inches apart.

CULTIVATION: Avoid all contact with plants when they are wet. Beans are shallow rooted, so weeds should be scraped away. Mulch is helpful, particularly in dry period.

HARVESTING: Shell beans are left on plants until pods are mature. Shell beans for immediate eating should be picked when beans are pushing out in the pod, but before pod has passed growth stage and begun to turn limp or to dry. For drying beans, cut and dry mature plants, then thrash or shell out beans, dry them.

ENEMIES: Buy the egg cases of preying mantis and introduce this hungry insect to your garden to feast on any Mexican bean beetles (and many other insects) that may trouble your crops. Also, to avoid this beetle, set out nasturtiums or garlic nearby. Rotenone can be sprinkled on bean plants. By purchasing resistant strains, staying out of the garden when plants are wet and having a bit of luck, the gardener can avoid the fungus diseases. Woodchucks appreciate newly sprouted beans.

VARIETIES: *French Horticulture* (68 days to harvest. Good producer). *Dwarf Horticulture* (65 days. Good green or dried). *Red Kidney* (95 days. Large beans. Good for variety of recipes, including baked, boiled and in soups).

19	VARIETY	DATE PLANTED	AMOUNT PLANTED (ROW LENGTH)
1.			
2.			
3.			

HARVEST DATES	VARIETY	EXPECTED	ACTUAL
1.			
2.			
3.			

SATISFIED WITH VARIETY, AMOUNT?

1. ______
2. ______
3. ______

NOTES ______

19	VARIETY	DATE PLANTED	AMOUNT PLANTED (ROW LENGTH)
1.			
2.			
3.			

HARVEST DATES	VARIETY	EXPECTED	ACTUAL
1.			
2.			
3.			

SATISFIED WITH VARIETY, AMOUNT?

1. ______
2. ______
3. ______

NOTES ______

19	VARIETY	DATE PLANTED	AMOUNT PLANTED (ROW LENGTH)
1.			
2.			
3.			

HARVEST DATES	VARIETY	EXPECTED	ACTUAL
1.			
2.			
3.			

SATISFIED WITH VARIETY, AMOUNT?

1. ______
2. ______
3. ______

NOTES ______

BEANS, LIMA, BUSH *(Phaseolus limensis)* Do best where summers are long and hot, and night temperatures remain above 50° for two months. Thus they are difficult to raise in northern United States. Can be used green or dried. Need fertile, well-drained mellow soils, not heavy clays, and soil should be improved with compost dug into rows. Half-pound of seeds for 50-foot row will yield 25 pounds of pods.

PLANTING: Dust seed with nitrogen inoculant. Plant lima beans week or more after date of average last spring frost, when soil has warmed to 65 degrees. Seed planted too early will rot. Put seeds eye down 4-6 inches apart, one inch deep in rows 24-30 inches apart. Cover with light soil that will not bake and prevent seedlings from forcing their way to surface.

CULTIVATION: Avoid contact with wet plants. Beans are shallow-rooted so do not cultivate deeply. Mulch is helpful, particularly in dry weather. Limas need a lot of moisture, so weekly watering may be needed in drought periods.

HARVESTING: Pick vines clean to promote bearing. Pods are ready for picking when beans have reached full size but pods have not yet turned yellow. If late crop is large, gardener may leave limas on vine until after frost, then pick. They will keep in shells for several weeks. Better method is to pull vines, dry them, then shell beans, or thresh them out by walking on dried vines.

ENEMIES: If weather is cold and wet at harvest time, downy mildew may cover pods with white patches. Burn those vines.

VARIETIES: Limas are small seeded and large seeded, and different varieties are popular in different areas. **Fordhook 242* (75 days to harvest. Large beans. Heat resistant) is most popular for main crop. In South, **Henderson* (65 days. Small seed) is old standby. In North, Dixie Butterpea (75 days, small-seeded, heavy crop) is popular.

In northern areas, where limas can't be grown, the *Fava Bean,* sometimes called *English Broad Bean,* is sometimes substituted. Extremely hardy, it can be planted when ground can be worked, before date of last frost. Plants yield in 85 days, with 7-inch pods containing 5-7 light green beans that look like limas but taste more like peas. Twelve ounces of seed needed for 50-foot row.

19	VARIETY	DATE PLANTED	AMOUNT PLANTED (ROW LENGTH)
1.			
2.			
3.			

HARVEST DATES	VARIETY	EXPECTED	ACTUAL
1.			
2.			
3.			

SATISFIED WITH VARIETY, AMOUNT?

1.
2.
3.

NOTES

19	VARIETY	DATE PLANTED	AMOUNT PLANTED (ROW LENGTH)
1.			
2.			
3.			

HARVEST DATES	VARIETY	EXPECTED	ACTUAL
1.			
2.			
3.			

SATISFIED WITH VARIETY, AMOUNT?

1.
2.
3.

NOTES

19	VARIETY	DATE PLANTED	AMOUNT PLANTED (ROW LENGTH)
1.			
2.			
3.			

HARVEST DATES	VARIETY	EXPECTED	ACTUAL
1.			
2.			
3.			

SATISFIED WITH VARIETY, AMOUNT?

1.
2.
3.

NOTES

BEANS, LIMA, POLE *(Phaseolus limensis)* Experienced gardeners find these produce a heavier crop of more flavorful beans than the bush limas. They are more difficult to grow, need a longer season than bush beans, but are freer of fungus diseases. Excellent green or dried and good for freezing. Poles should be set at north side of garden, to avoid shading other crops. They require a long, hot summer, with a minimum of two months in which night temperatures remain above 50°, so are not practical for northern United States. Avoid clay soils. These do best in fertile, well-drained mellow soil. Four ounces of seed needed for 50-foot row of hills set 36 inches apart, and will yield 25 pounds of pods.

PLANTING: Dust seed with nitrogen inoculant. These can be grown on five-foot fence, on trellises made of heavy twine, or on 10-foot poles with bark still on them. Set poles individually, three feet into ground and three feet apart, or form tripod of poles, three feet apart at base. Two weeks after last spring frost, plant seeds eye downward one inch deep, eight inches apart along fence or trellis. On poles, plant six seeds to each pole, thin to three plants each.

CULTIVATION: Avoid touching wet plants. Beans are shallow rooted so do not cultivate deeply. Mulch heavily, particularly in dry weather. Weekly watering may be needed in period of drought.

HARVESTING: They are hard to shell when small and you will get few beans, but try a few while they are still green and before the pods fill out. They're delicious. Will yield until frost. In general, pick when beans begin to bulge in pods, since they will toughen later. If late crop is heavy, gardener can pick after first light frost. They will keep in shells for several weeks. Or he may pull vines and dry them, then shell beans.

ENEMIES: Limas, if weather is cold and wet at harvesting time, may be hit by downy mildew that covers pods with white patches. Burn these vines.

VARIETIES: **King of the Garden* (88 days. Heavy producer. Five-inch pods with 3-4 large flat beans in each pod. Will grow 8-10 feet tall). **Burpee's Best* (92 days. 4-5 inch pods, with 4-5 large, plump beans. Will grow 10-12 feet tall).

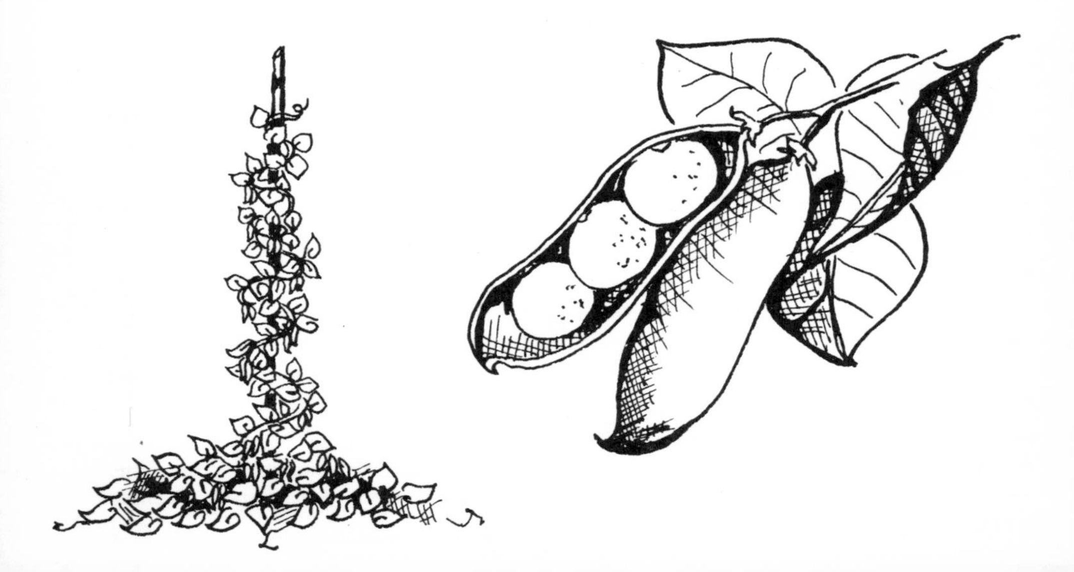

19	VARIETY	DATE PLANTED	AMOUNT PLANTED (ROW LENGTH)
1.			
2.			
3.			

HARVEST DATES	VARIETY	EXPECTED	ACTUAL
1.			
2.			
3.			

SATISFIED WITH VARIETY, AMOUNT?

1.
2.
3.

NOTES

19	VARIETY	DATE PLANTED	AMOUNT PLANTED (ROW LENGTH)
1.			
2.			
3.			

HARVEST DATES	VARIETY	EXPECTED	ACTUAL
1.			
2.			
3.			

SATISFIED WITH VARIETY, AMOUNT?

1.
2.
3.

NOTES

19	VARIETY	DATE PLANTED	AMOUNT PLANTED (ROW LENGTH)
1.			
2.			
3.			

HARVEST DATES	VARIETY	EXPECTED	ACTUAL
1.			
2.			
3.			

SATISFIED WITH VARIETY, AMOUNT?

1.
2.
3.

NOTES

BEANS, POLE *(Phaseolus vulgaris)* Try these at least once in your garden. They will grow throughout the United States, in many varieties. Generally they are the most productive, the most delicious of all beans. Also they are fun to grow, since they are one of the most spectacular crops, reaching impressive heights. Gardener should contain his enthusiasm for altitude, remembering that in achieving great heights through use of long poles he sacrifices ease of harvesting. Pole beans produce at later date than bush varieties, but crop is greater, tastier and grows in larger pods. These are satisfied with relatively poor soils. Place poles where they will not cast shadow over rest of garden. Two ounces of seed planted in 50 feet of 36-inch spaced hills will produce 25 pounds.

PLANTING: After date of last spring frost, set poles first. Ten-foot poles can be set three feet into ground, three feet apart, or poles can be set in tripod arrangement, three feet apart at base, and tied at top. Dust seeds with nitrogen inoculant. Sow 6-8 seeds per hill, one inch deep, and thin to four plants when four inches tall.

CULTIVATION: Avoid contact with wet plants. Do not cultivate deeply. Mulch is helpful, particularly in dry weather.

HARVESTING: Pick when pods are nearly full grown, but beans are not fully developed and pods are still crisp. If development has progressed beyond that, delay picking until full grown, for use as shell or dry beans, and be satisfied with second best.

ENEMIES: Chief among them is the Mexican bean beetle. Introduce preying mantis to prey on them. Also plant garlic in each hill of beans. Dust with rotenone. And if these don't work, pick the little pests and destroy the eggs laid on underside of leaves. Select resistant seeds if rusts or other diseases are problem. Watch newly-emerged bean plants if woodchucks frequent your area.

VARIETIES: Old-time favorites are **Kentucky Wonder* (65 days to harvest. Green beans. Heavy producer and good for both snap beans and shell beans) and **Kentucky Wonder Wax* (68 days. Waxy yellow and good for snap and shell beans). **Blue Lake* (60 days. Straight, dark green, and good fresh, canned or frozen). *Romano* (70 days. A popular Italian pole bean with distinctive flavor and flat pods).

19	VARIETY	DATE PLANTED	AMOUNT PLANTED (ROW LENGTH)
1.			
2.			
3.			

HARVEST DATES	VARIETY	EXPECTED	ACTUAL
1.			
2.			
3.			

SATISFIED WITH VARIETY, AMOUNT?

1.
2.
3.

NOTES

19	VARIETY	DATE PLANTED	AMOUNT PLANTED (ROW LENGTH)
1.			
2.			
3.			

HARVEST DATES	VARIETY	EXPECTED	ACTUAL
1.			
2.			
3.			

SATISFIED WITH VARIETY, AMOUNT?

1.
2.
3.

NOTES

19	VARIETY	DATE PLANTED	AMOUNT PLANTED (ROW LENGTH)
1.			
2.			
3.			

HARVEST DATES	VARIETY	EXPECTED	ACTUAL
1.			
2.			
3.			

SATISFIED WITH VARIETY, AMOUNT?

1.
2.
3.

NOTES

BEETS *(Beta vulgaris)* Raised throughout the United States. Cold-hardy and easy to grow. Resistant to insects and diseases. Should have sunny, sandy loam site, with compost well dug in. Roots and early greens are eaten. Fall crop can be stored. Half-ounce of seed for 50-foot row will yield about 50 pounds.

PLANTING: Seeds are in clumps of three or four seeds, so sow sparsely, one-two inches apart, four weeks before last spring frost, or as early as soil can be worked. Space rows 12-18 inches apart. Cover seeds with half-inch of fine soil. When four inches tall, thin beets to stand two-three inches apart, and use thinnings for transplants or for tasty greens. Don't fertilize with fresh manure. Mulch seedlings heavily. Start successive plantings two-three weeks apart for continuing supply. For fall and storage crop, plant six-eight weeks before first fall frost.

HARVESTING: Harvest begins when roots are 1-1½ inches in diameter and at their best. Beets are tastiest before reaching maturity, and become woody if left in ground after maturity. When harvesting, leave inch or two of stems attached to roots to avoid bleeding. For winter storage, leave beets in ground until after first light frosts, then store in cold (35°-40°), high humidity. Boxes of moist sand are ideal for storage. Beets are easily canned or frozen, a treat when pickled.

VARIETIES: For early crop, try *Early Wonder* (55 days to harvest, flattened, globe shaped) and **Crosby's Egyptian* (56 days, dark red, tasty). For later crop and fall planting for storage, **Detroit Dark Red* (60 days, dark red and sweet). *Lutz Green Leaf* (80 days. Can be used either small or large, and is a good winter keeper).

19	VARIETY	DATE PLANTED	AMOUNT PLANTED (ROW LENGTH)
1.			
2.			
3.			

HARVEST DATES	VARIETY	EXPECTED	ACTUAL
1.			
2.			
3.			

SATISFIED WITH VARIETY, AMOUNT?

1. ____
2. ____
3. ____

NOTES ____

19	VARIETY	DATE PLANTED	AMOUNT PLANTED (ROW LENGTH)
1.			
2.			
3.			

HARVEST DATES	VARIETY	EXPECTED	ACTUAL
1.			
2.			
3.			

SATISFIED WITH VARIETY, AMOUNT?

1. ____
2. ____
3. ____

NOTES ____

19	VARIETY	DATE PLANTED	AMOUNT PLANTED (ROW LENGTH)
1.			
2.			
3.			

HARVEST DATES	VARIETY	EXPECTED	ACTUAL
1.			
2.			
3.			

SATISFIED WITH VARIETY, AMOUNT?

1. ____
2. ____
3. ____

NOTES ____

BROCCOLI *(Brassica oleracea italica)* A delicately-flavored member of the cabbage family, grown throughout United States. Common in American gardens only during this century. A good source of vitamins A, B and C. Requires rich, loose soil that holds moisture, and with compost added. Will stand cold. Raised as spring or fall crop, with fall crop heavier. Spring crop of 25 transplants in 50-foot row will yield 25 pounds, more than most families will want.

PLANTING: For spring planting, start plants indoors 5-6 weeks before time to set them out, which is as soon as soil can be worked, and before date of last frost. On cloudy day, set them 24 inches apart, in rows three feet apart. If cutworms are problem, protect seedlings with paper collars. For fall crop, which will continue growth after first frost, sow seeds in garden in early summer. Transplant thinnings to another row. This row will be delayed for several weeks by transplanting, thus spreading out period of harvest.

CULTIVATION: Shallow, to avoid damage to roots. Mulch to preserve moisture, since plants need continuing supply. Side-dressing of high-nitrogen fertilizer, such as blood meal, good if dug in about 15 days after plants are set out, again when heads begin to form.

HARVESTING: Broccoli is grown for its flower-bud clusters, and tender stems and leaves near them. Cut clusters with a 4-6 inch stalk before flowers open. After first large central cluster is cut, smaller clusters will form in leaf axils, which also may be harvested. Broccoli freezes well. A small, green larva is often found imbedded in broccoli that has been harvested. Several soakings in salt water will remove it.

ENEMIES: Cabbage worm. This is the green larva of a white butterfly that is seen fluttering in seemingly innocent abandon over members of the cabbage family. Hand pick worms, searching plants carefully for them. Companion plant with chives or garlic. Dust crop with salt when plants are wet. If these fail, dust with rotenone. To halt maggots, place square of tarpaper around base of young plant. Aphids are repelled by nasturtiums, devoured by ladybugs. Most diseases can be avoided by buying good seed, maintaining rich soil and avoiding the planting of cabbage family members in the same location more often than once every four years. Persons who buy rather than starting their own broccoli plants often purchase trouble too.

VARIETIES: **Italian Green Sprouting* (70 days from time of transplant to harvest. Medium early with dark blue-green heads of good quality). *Spartan Early* (76 days. Compact plants). **De Cicco—Burpee's Greensbud Brand* (60 days. Early. Deep color).

19 VARIETY	DATE PLANTED	AMOUNT PLANTED (ROW LENGTH)
1.		
2.		
3.		

HARVEST DATES VARIETY	EXPECTED	ACTUAL
1.		
2.		
3.		

SATISFIED WITH VARIETY, AMOUNT?

1.
2.
3.

NOTES

19 VARIETY	DATE PLANTED	AMOUNT PLANTED (ROW LENGTH)
1.		
2.		
3.		

HARVEST DATES VARIETY	EXPECTED	ACTUAL
1.		
2.		
3.		

SATISFIED WITH VARIETY, AMOUNT?

1.
2.
3.

NOTES

19 VARIETY	DATE PLANTED	AMOUNT PLANTED (ROW LENGTH)
1.		
2.		
3.		

HARVEST DATES VARIETY	EXPECTED	ACTUAL
1.		
2.		
3.		

SATISFIED WITH VARIETY, AMOUNT?

1.
2.
3.

NOTES

BRUSSELS SPROUTS *(Brassica oleracea bullata gemmifera)* Easy to raise, and improved by a few fall frosts. More hardy than cabbage. Will live through winter in milder climates, so are grown as winter crop in South, late fall crop in North. Twenty-five plants in 50-foot row will yield 25 pounds.

PLANTING: Take pencil in hand to decide on correct date for starting sprouts indoors. Allow 50-75 days from date of seeding to date of transplanting, when they are 7-8 inches tall, plus 75 days from transplanting to mature plants. Thus in many areas where Brussels sprouts are raised as fall crop, seeds are started in mid-May, are ready to transplant about Aug. 1 and will be ready for first harvesting about Oct. 15. If Brussels sprouts are started too early, so that they mature in warm weather, the sprouts will not be tight and tasty, but will be loose-leafed and a fit contribution, not to the kitchen but to the compost pile. When transplanting into the garden, try to pick a cloudy day, and place plants 24 inches apart in rows 24-30 inches apart.

CULTIVATION: Need lot of moisture so mulch heavily. Because roots are near surface, restrained cultivation is advised. Nitrogenous fertilizer such as blood meal, cottonseed meal or fish meal should be used as side dressing 2-3 weeks after plants are set out, again when sprouts are forming. As sprouts form at base of plant, and leaves begin to yellow, remove these leaves to give sprouts ample room. Don't remove upper leaves. In early fall, pinch off tops of plants. This will reduce total crop, but speed development of sprouts.

HARVESTING: Beginning at bottom of plant, as sprouts reach about one inch in diameter, twist sprouts off stalk. Those picked after frost are tastier. If crop has not been completely harvested before danger of heavy frost, plants can be pulled, stored for protection against freezing, with roots kept damp. This will continue the harvest for as much as a month.

ENEMIES: If yellow jackets are seen around cabbage-family plants, they are not enemies, since they will do away with cabbage worms. Another method is to mix a handful of wood ashes, a handful of lime and two gallons of water, and spray mixture on the plants. Also can be hand picked or dusted with rotenone. Don't raise members of cabbage family in same location more than once every four years, to avoid diseases.

VARIETIES: **Jade Cross* (80 days from time of transplant to harvest. Uniform, firm sprouts). **Long Island* Improved-Catskill strain (90 days. Tight heads).

19	VARIETY	DATE PLANTED	AMOUNT PLANTED (ROW LENGTH)
1.			
2.			
3.			

HARVEST DATES	VARIETY	EXPECTED	ACTUAL
1.			
2.			
3.			

SATISFIED WITH VARIETY, AMOUNT?

1.
2.
3.

NOTES

19	VARIETY	DATE PLANTED	AMOUNT PLANTED (ROW LENGTH)
1.			
2.			
3.			

HARVEST DATES	VARIETY	EXPECTED	ACTUAL
1.			
2.			
3.			

SATISFIED WITH VARIETY, AMOUNT?

1.
2.
3.

NOTES

19	VARIETY	DATE PLANTED	AMOUNT PLANTED (ROW LENGTH)
1.			
2.			
3.			

HARVEST DATES	VARIETY	EXPECTED	ACTUAL
1.			
2.			
3.			

SATISFIED WITH VARIETY, AMOUNT?

1.
2.
3.

NOTES

CABBAGE *(Brassica oleracea capitata)* Grown in cool weather throughout United States, as winter crop in South, spring and fall crop in the North. Gardener has choice of green-foliaged, red or Savoy cabbage, in early, mid-season and late varieties and should experiment. Heads are beautiful enough for the flower garden. Rich, moist soil, with compost added for this heavy eater. 25 plants in 50-foot row.

PLANTING: For spring crop, start transplants of early varieties indoors, 6-8 weeks in advance. Harden gradually, then set out as soon as ground can be worked. Set 18-24 inches apart, in rows 18-24 inches apart. Late cabbage can follow such crops as peas, beans and spinach, from transplants started in open seed beds. Those need more room, setting out two feet apart in rows 30-36 inches apart. Transplant early enough to mature by average date of first fall frost, but should be gathered only after early frost.

HARVESTING: Pick early cabbages as needed, before plants reach full maturity. Fall cabbages improved by light frost, but should be harvested before heavy freeze. To store, pull heads with roots, place them head down on bed of straw, hay or dry leaves, cover with heavy layer of this packing material. This can be in unheated building or outside, and cabbages will keep until well into winter.

ENEMIES: A recital of all that may happen to cabbages between time of transplanting and of harvesting would discourage most beginners from trying to raise them. A good crop is generally assured if the soil is good, plants are free of disease, the moisture supply is adequate and the cabbages receive good supply of compost and are well mulched. Cabbage worm: This is the green larva of a white butterfly seen around cabbages. Hand pick worms, searching plants carefully for them. Companion plant with chives or garlic. Dust crop with salt when plants are wet. If these fail, dust with rotenone. If cabbage maggot is a known danger, place a square of tarpaper around the base of each plant as it is set out. If ricelike eggs are found at base of plant, this is a warning that maggots are soon to hatch. Dig in handful of wood ashes around each plant. Aphids may be repelled by nasturtiums, washed off with hose, devoured by lady bugs. Avoid planting any member of the cabbage family in the same location more than once every four years.

VARIETIES, EARLY: *Burpee's Copenhagen Market* (72 days from transplants to maturity, 4-4½ pound heads). *Emerald Cross* (69 days, early hybrid, 4-6 pound heads). *Golden Acre* (64 days, 4-5 pound heads).

MIDSEASON,(which is usually most difficult period to grow cabbage): *Stonehead,* (67 days, 4-pound heads).

LATE: *Danish Ballhead* (105 days, round, very firm heads). *Eastern Ballhead* (95 days, 6-7 pound heads).

RED CABBAGE: (very worth trying) *Resistant Red Acre* (76 days, deep red, good for early yield). *Mammoth Red Rock* (100 days, deep purple-red heads 6-8 pounds).

SAVOY: *Perfection Drumhead* (90 days, green heads weighting 6-7 pounds). *Savoy King* (90 days. Good fall crop with four-pound semiflat heads).

19	VARIETY	DATE PLANTED	AMOUNT PLANTED (ROW LENGTH)
1.			
2.			
3.			

HARVEST DATES	VARIETY	EXPECTED	ACTUAL
1.			
2.			
3.			

SATISFIED WITH VARIETY, AMOUNT?

1.
2.
3.

NOTES

19	VARIETY	DATE PLANTED	AMOUNT PLANTED (ROW LENGTH)
1.			
2.			
3.			

HARVEST DATES	VARIETY	EXPECTED	ACTUAL
1.			
2.			
3.			

SATISFIED WITH VARIETY, AMOUNT?

1.
2.
3.

NOTES

19	VARIETY	DATE PLANTED	AMOUNT PLANTED (ROW LENGTH)
1.			
2.			
3.			

HARVEST DATES	VARIETY	EXPECTED	ACTUAL
1.			
2.			
3.			

SATISFIED WITH VARIETY, AMOUNT?

1.
2.
3.

NOTES

CARROTS *(Daucus carota)* Grown in fall, winter and spring in South, throughout summer in North. A gardener's common error is to grow far too many summer squashes, far too few carrots. Housewives will use many carrots in cooking soups, stews and other dishes, and in salads. Small carrots freeze well, and are handy for the cook throughout winter. Carrots are at their best when half-grown or smaller, a size rarely found in the supermarket. Plant more than you think you will want but in succession plantings. Grow best in rich, mellow, deeply worked soil that is free from clods and stones. Avoid using fresh manure; it makes carrots rough-skinned. Use compost instead. A ⅛-½ ounce packet of seed in 50-foot row will yield 50 pounds of carrots.

PLANTING: As soon as ground can be prepared, sow thinly, covering with half-inch of fine soil that will not bake to crust. Drop in a few radish seeds to mark the row, since carrots germinate at a leisurely pace. Rows are 12-18 inches apart. Make successive plantings at two-week intervals. Carrots may be planted in rows of cabbage or Brussels sprouts, and harvested before other crops need the space.

CULTIVATING: It's slow work but worth it to hand pick weeds from row to avoid weeds crowding out slowly emerging carrot tops. Mulch when tops are four inches high.

HARVESTING: Harvesting and thinning are same operation. When carrots reach half-inch in diameter, they are delicious, so can be harvested, to leave three inches between those remaining. Carrots in ground from latter plantings can be blanketed under heavy layer of hay, dug up as needed during winter. Or, after first frost, they may be dug, all but inch of tops cut off, and stored in cool, humid cellar, or buried in damp sand in boxes in cool spot. But they are much more handy when ready for action in the freezer.

ENEMIES: Usually enemy free. If tiny holes are found bored in root, it is the work of the larvae of the carrot rust fly. Avoid planting where celery or carrots were grown previously, and sprinkle wood ashes in row. If problem has been a continuing one, avoid planting an early crop of carrots (and celery) for one year. A crop planted after June 1 will avoid the larva cycle of this fly.

VARIETIES: Long, slim varieties grow best in sandy soil; chunky varieties in heavier soil. **Chantenay Long* (60 days to maturity. Long end tapered) **Nantes Half-Long* (75 days. Slim and cylindrical). *Short' Sweet* (68 days. Will grow in heavy soil).

19	VARIETY	DATE PLANTED	AMOUNT PLANTED (ROW LENGTH)
1.			
2.			
3.			

HARVEST DATES	VARIETY	EXPECTED	ACTUAL
1.			
2.			
3.			

SATISFIED WITH VARIETY, AMOUNT?

1.
2.
3.

NOTES

19	VARIETY	DATE PLANTED	AMOUNT PLANTED (ROW LENGTH)
1.			
2.			
3.			

HARVEST DATES	VARIETY	EXPECTED	ACTUAL
1.			
2.			
3.			

SATISFIED WITH VARIETY, AMOUNT?

1.
2.
3.

NOTES

19	VARIETY	DATE PLANTED	AMOUNT PLANTED (ROW LENGTH)
1.			
2.			
3.			

HARVEST DATES	VARIETY	EXPECTED	ACTUAL
1.			
2.			
3.			

SATISFIED WITH VARIETY, AMOUNT?

1.
2.
3.

NOTES

CAULIFLOWER *(Brassica oleracea botrytis)* Fussiest of cabbage family to grow. Requires well-limed soil, abundance of organic material, cool temperatures, ample supply of moisture, ample fertilizer—and a little luck. Twenty-five plants in 50-foot row.

PLANTING: Start plants indoors, five weeks in advance. Set out when transplants are six inches tall, about date of last spring frost, two feet apart in rows three feet apart, then water well. Avoid disturbing roots. For later crop, sow seeds in garden in the late spring, early summer. Transplant on cloudy day, or shade transplants. To save space, plant carrots, onions or radishes between plants, harvest them before cauliflowers need space.

CULTIVATION: Cultivate lightly. Mulch heavily to keep plants cool, avoid loss of moisture. Fertilize every three-four weeks. When cauliflower clusters are two inches in diameter, pull a few of the plant's leaves over them, tie them loosely, to blanch heads. Keep well watered after this. Purple varieties are not blanched.

HARVESTING: Don't delay harvesting when cauliflowers are ready or they will pass their peak. About a week after tying, head should be developed enough to be cut. To save maturing fall crop before heavy frost, pull entire plants, put them tightly together in cold frame or unheated building, use as needed.

ENEMIES: Put paper collars around transplants to avoid cutworm damage. Cabbage worm can be picked off or can be discouraged with companion planting of chives or garlic; dusted when wet with salt, or dusted with rotenone. Scatter wood ashes around base to discourage maggots. Avoid planting this or any other members of cabbage family in same location more than once every four years.

VARIETIES: *Early Snowball A* (60 days from transplant to maturity) **Burpeeana* (58 days. *Super Snowball* variety. Dependable).

19 VARIETY	DATE PLANTED	AMOUNT PLANTED (ROW LENGTH)
1.		
2.		
3.		

HARVEST DATES VARIETY	EXPECTED	ACTUAL
1.		
2.		
3.		

SATISFIED WITH VARIETY, AMOUNT?

1.
2.
3.

NOTES

19 VARIETY	DATE PLANTED	AMOUNT PLANTED (ROW LENGTH)
1.		
2.		
3.		

HARVEST DATES VARIETY	EXPECTED	ACTUAL
1.		
2.		
3.		

SATISFIED WITH VARIETY, AMOUNT?

1.
2.
3.

NOTES

19 VARIETY	DATE PLANTED	AMOUNT PLANTED (ROW LENGTH)
1.		
2.		
3.		

HARVEST DATES VARIETY	EXPECTED	ACTUAL
1.		
2.		
3.		

SATISFIED WITH VARIETY, AMOUNT?

1.
2.
3.

NOTES

CELERY *(Apium graveolens)* Can be grown throughout United States, as a winter crop in the deep South, early spring or late fall crop further north, and a late summer crop in the North. Rich, moist soil should be prepared with quantity of rotted manure or compost worked into row. One hundred plants per 50-foot row.

PLANTING: It is essential that seeds be started indoors 10 weeks in advance of transplanting into garden. Seeds can be placed in cloth bag, soaked overnight, then mixed with dry sand and planted in seed flats, covered with half-inch of leafmold or similar material. Seed requires 10-15 days in 65-degree soil to germinate. Cover flats with damp burlap to keep seeds moist. Transplant once to separate them into two-inch squares, or into three-inch peat pots, before moving them outdoors. They should be placed in garden several weeks after last spring frost, when night temperatures aren't expected to drop below 40°. Plant six inches apart, in double rows 12 inches apart. Keep double rows 24 inches apart. After transplanting, water plants and shade them for several days if sunny.

CULTIVATION: Mulch heavily to keep soil moist and plants cool. Add mulch as plants grow upward. This helps to keep plants erect.

HARVESTING: If blanched celery is desired, boards about a foot wide should be placed on either side of rows, covering all but top six inches of plants, and held in place by shoveling soil up against them. Blanching requires about two weeks. Plants may be harvested as required from the time they reach two-thirds of their growth. Plants may be stored in the rows where they grew by placing a layer of dry straw or hay over them, while blanching boards are still in place. Or plants may be pulled, stored closely together in boxes, and kept in unheated building.

ENEMIES: Damping off is the greatest problem, in warm, wet weather. Keep rows weed-free to avoid spread of virus diseases by aphids.

VARIETIES: *Giant Pascal* (135 days from date plants are placed in garden). *Fordhook* (130 days, good for fall, winter storage).

CELERIAC or root celery is grown exactly like celery, but is raised for its turnip-shaped roots which are edible at any stage. Good in soup, stews, other dishes.

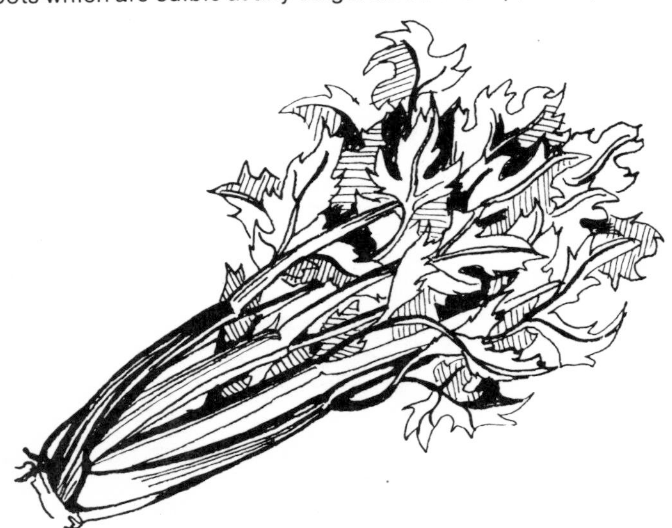

19	VARIETY	DATE PLANTED	AMOUNT PLANTED (ROW LENGTH)
1.			
2.			
3.			

HARVEST DATES	VARIETY	EXPECTED	ACTUAL
1.			
2.			
3.			

SATISFIED WITH VARIETY, AMOUNT?

1.
2.
3.

NOTES

19	VARIETY	DATE PLANTED	AMOUNT PLANTED (ROW LENGTH)
1.			
2.			
3.			

HARVEST DATES	VARIETY	EXPECTED	ACTUAL
1.			
2.			
3.			

SATISFIED WITH VARIETY, AMOUNT?

1.
2.
3.

NOTES

19	VARIETY	DATE PLANTED	AMOUNT PLANTED (ROW LENGTH)
1.			
2.			
3.			

HARVEST DATES	VARIETY	EXPECTED	ACTUAL
1.			
2.			
3.			

SATISFIED WITH VARIETY, AMOUNT?

1.
2.
3.

NOTES

CHICORY *(Cichorium intybus)* Will grow throughout United States, and grows wild in many areas, especially along highways, having escaped cultivation. It is grown for several purposes. The young tops are eaten as greens, the roots are roasted, ground and mixed with coffee, particularly in the South, and the roots are sometimes cooked and eaten like carrots and turnips. The home gardener will raise witloof chicory, sometimes called either French endive or Belgian endive. This variety is grown primarily to produce roots which are stored, then forced in winter to produce large, tender white sprouts or heads used for salads. Gourmets will find this lengthy effort worthwhile. Deep, rich soil without too much organic matter. Quarter-ounce of seed in 50-foot row will produce 100 roots.

PLANTING: In late spring or early summer, sow seeds sparsely, with seeds half-inch deep in rows 24 inches apart. Thin plants to six inches apart to give room for root development.

CULTIVATION: Plants will grow 2-4 feet high with little assistance. Mulching recommended to restrain weeds.

HARVESTING: After first killing frost, dig up roots, cut off tops to within an inch of crowns, and, for uniform size, cut off all below a nine-inch section. Store roots in box filled with damp sand or soil and store in near-freezing temperature. Roots should be covered with six-inch layer of sand or soil. Three weeks before shoots are desired, box should be moved into dark cellar, with temperature at about 60°, and with topping of sand remaining in place. Contents should be watered weekly. In about three weeks, 5-6 inch heads resembling Cos lettuce will develop. After cutting, roots are discarded.

19	VARIETY	DATE PLANTED	AMOUNT PLANTED (ROW LENGTH)
1.			
2.			
3.			
HARVEST DATES	VARIETY	EXPECTED	ACTUAL
1.			
2.			
3.			
SATISFIED WITH VARIETY, AMOUNT?			
1.			
2.			
3.			

NOTES

19	VARIETY	DATE PLANTED	AMOUNT PLANTED (ROW LENGTH)
1.			
2.			
3.			
HARVEST DATES	VARIETY	EXPECTED	ACTUAL
1.			
2.			
3.			
SATISFIED WITH VARIETY, AMOUNT?			
1.			
2.			
3.			

NOTES

19	VARIETY	DATE PLANTED	AMOUNT PLANTED (ROW LENGTH)
1.			
2.			
3.			
HARVEST DATES	VARIETY	EXPECTED	ACTUAL
1.			
2.			
3.			
SATISFIED WITH VARIETY, AMOUNT?			
1.			
2.			
3.			

NOTES

CHINESE CABBAGE *(Brassica pekinensis)* Deserves greater popularity than it has. May be used like lettuce. Best raised in fall in North, in winter in South. Needs rich, moist soil. Quarter-ounce of seed in 50-foot row will produce 40 heads.

PLANTING: Can be started indoors, but the better method in the North is to seed directly into garden about 75-80 days before first fall frost is expected. In South, plantings can start month before first cool weather of fall, continue until 75-80 days before hot weather of early summer. Dig compost into seedbed, place seeds 6-8 inches apart, cover with sifted compost. Rows should be 30 inches apart. Thin to 12-16 inches apart when plants are 6-8 inches high, and use thinnings for cooked greens or in salads.

CULTIVATION: Keep mulch around them and maintain moisture in soil.

HARVESTING: As heads mature, cut them. If outer leaves are tough, remove them. Heads may be used in salads, cooked as cabbage, shredded for cole slaw. Untrimmed heads may be refrigerated for a month, or stored an equal time in layers of straw in unheated building.

ENEMIES: All of those associated with the cabbage family. Try doing in the cabbage worm by interplanting chives and garlic. A scattering of wood ashes scratched lightly around soil at base of plants may keep off the maggots. Avoid planting this or any other members of cabbage family in same location more than once every four years.

VARIETIES: *Michihli* (70 days to harvest. Distinctive, pleasing flavor).

19 VARIETY	DATE PLANTED	AMOUNT PLANTED (ROW LENGTH)
1.		
2.		
3.		

HARVEST DATES VARIETY	EXPECTED	ACTUAL
1.		
2.		
3.		

SATISFIED WITH VARIETY, AMOUNT?

1.
2.
3.

NOTES

19 VARIETY	DATE PLANTED	AMOUNT PLANTED (ROW LENGTH)
1.		
2.		
3.		

HARVEST DATES VARIETY	EXPECTED	ACTUAL
1.		
2.		
3.		

SATISFIED WITH VARIETY, AMOUNT?

1.
2.
3.

NOTES

19 VARIETY	DATE PLANTED	AMOUNT PLANTED (ROW LENGTH)
1.		
2.		
3.		

HARVEST DATES VARIETY	EXPECTED	ACTUAL
1.		
2.		
3.		

SATISFIED WITH VARIETY, AMOUNT?

1.
2.
3.

NOTES

CHIVES *(Allium schoenoprasum)* Perennial. Make room in every garden, no matter how small, for this delicate flavored but hardy member of the onion family. A clump will take up only a square foot of space, and provide the chives a housewife will use almost daily. Plant them as handy as possible to the kitchen door, even if this means crowding a clump or two into a flower bed. Chives will grow anywhere in the United States, and anywhere in the garden, but are best where they are handy for use, yet won't be in the way in preparation of the garden for annual crops.

SEEDING: Fresh seeds are a must, since these remain viable for only a year. Plant either in pots or directly into garden, planting in small clumps. Easier method of starting new clumps is to divide two-three-year-old ones. Small clumps of chives frequently used in border, or scattered throughout garden to discourage many harmful insects.

CULTIVATION: Only need feeding if plants weaken. Clumps usually grow tightly enough together to squeeze out weeds.

HARVESTING: Cut tops whenever needed, for salads, mixed with cottage cheese, added to soups and stews, and in many other ways. Such cutting stimulates further growth. Chives should be potted in fall, left outside until needed in kitchen, then brought in, where they will quickly resume growth.

19	VARIETY	DATE PLANTED	AMOUNT PLANTED (ROW LENGTH)
1.			
2.			
3.			

HARVEST DATES	VARIETY	EXPECTED	ACTUAL
1.			
2.			
3.			

SATISFIED WITH VARIETY, AMOUNT?

1.
2.
3.

NOTES

19	VARIETY	DATE PLANTED	AMOUNT PLANTED (ROW LENGTH)
1.			
2.			
3.			

HARVEST DATES	VARIETY	EXPECTED	ACTUAL
1.			
2.			
3.			

SATISFIED WITH VARIETY, AMOUNT?

1.
2.
3.

NOTES

19	VARIETY	DATE PLANTED	AMOUNT PLANTED (ROW LENGTH)
1.			
2.			
3.			

HARVEST DATES	VARIETY	EXPECTED	ACTUAL
1.			
2.			
3.			

SATISFIED WITH VARIETY, AMOUNT?

1.
2.
3.

NOTES

COLLARDS *(Brassica oleracea acephala)* These are the botanical Stars and Bars as symbols of the South, and they are rarely seen in the North. They are particularly popular in hot areas, where crops of cabbage would fail. Twenty-five full-grown plants in 50-foot row will yield more collards than most families will want, even if their names are Lee and Jeff Davis.

PLANTING: In North, when ground can be worked, and in South, either in spring or in fall, plant seed thinly and half-inch deep, in rows three feet apart. Using thinnings in salads or cooked as greens, thin later to stand three inches apart, thin again to six inches apart, and finally 24 inches apart. Collards grow as high as four feet.

CULTIVATION: Strive for rapid growth by working compost or manure into seedbed, and by mulching crop. Shallow cultivation advised to avoid cutting roots.

HARVESTING: Fleshy leaves are picked before they reach full size. Do not pick or damage central bud, or growth of plant will be halted. Light frosts improve flavor of collards.

ENEMIES: Cabbage worm can be picked off or can be discouraged with companion planting of chives or garlic, dusted with rotenone. Scatter wood ashes around base to discourage maggots. Avoid planting this or any other members of cabbage family in same location more than once every four years.

VARIETIES: *Georgia* (80 days to harvesting. Mild). *Vates* (80 days. More compact.)

19	VARIETY	DATE PLANTED	AMOUNT PLANTED (ROW LENGTH)
1.			
2.			
3.			

HARVEST DATES	VARIETY	EXPECTED	ACTUAL
1.			
2.			
3.			

SATISFIED WITH VARIETY, AMOUNT?

1.
2.
3.

NOTES

19	VARIETY	DATE PLANTED	AMOUNT PLANTED (ROW LENGTH)
1.			
2.			
3.			

HARVEST DATES	VARIETY	EXPECTED	ACTUAL
1.			
2.			
3.			

SATISFIED WITH VARIETY, AMOUNT?

1.
2.
3.

NOTES

19	VARIETY	DATE PLANTED	AMOUNT PLANTED (ROW LENGTH)
1.			
2.			
3.			

HARVEST DATES	VARIETY	EXPECTED	ACTUAL
1.			
2.			
3.			

SATISFIED WITH VARIETY, AMOUNT?

1.
2.
3.

NOTES

CORN *(Zea mays)* One of best reasons for having a home garden. Takes much space, but worth it. Grows throughout United States. Requires fertile, well-drained but moist soil. Dig compost or well-rotted manure into soil for this heavy feeder. One ounce of seed for 50-foot row will yield 75 ears—not enough for a hungry family.

PLANTING: When danger of frost is past, and soil has warmed to 50 degrees, plant seeds one inch deep in rows or hills. In rows, preferable for home gardens, sow seed every 6-9 inches in rows 2-2½ feet apart. For hills, plant three seeds to hill, with hills two feet apart and rows 2-2½ feet apart. Plant each variety in four or more short adjoining rows, rather than one long row, for better pollination. Plan carefully and plant several varieties, with different planting dates, to assure steady supply over extended period. Days required for yield, as listed with each variety, helpful in this planning, or plant new row when first is up 2-3 inches. Plantings of hybrids, particularly, tend to ripen all at once.

HARVESTING: Pick corn only when ready to eat it. The common advice is to have water boiling before picking, to make delay between picking and eating as short as possible. Equally important is picking corn when it has reached proper development. Ears, when too immature to eat, have small kernels with watery juice. Next is milk stage, when kernels become plump. This is when corn should be eaten. Next is dough stage, when sugars have changed to starch. Pick when silks first become brown and ears feel full.

ENEMIES: Corn has enemies from day it is planted, and crows try to find sprouting seeds to eat, to the night it ripens to perfection, and racoons banquet on it. Other enemies: Corn borer overwinters on stubble and old stalks, so remove them from garden and compost them. Corn ear worm can be discouraged by drop of mineral oil in each developing ear.

VARIETIES: Experimenting is urged to match your growing conditions and your tastes to the best variety. Try both hybrids (more productive, but all in single planting will mature at once) and open-pollinated (sweeter, contain more protein) varieties. General rule is that varieties ripening later in season are tastier than the early ones. **Honeycross* (87 days to picking. Hybrid. Wilt-resistant. High yield). *Honey and Cream* (78 days. Favorite hybrid for many with its white and yellow kernels). *Silver Queen* (92 days. Hybrid. Tops for eating). *Spancross* (71 days. Very popular early hybrid). **Golden Bantam* (80 days. Open-pollinated. An old favorite, and deservedly so).

If there is extra room in garden, plant a few short rows of **POPCORN** seed. This corn, planted like sweet corn, must be permitted to mature. Dry ears, then shuck them. Popping it in winter will bring memories of sunny, warm days of gardening, and make popcorn doubly satisfying.

19	VARIETY	DATE PLANTED	AMOUNT PLANTED (ROW LENGTH)
1.			
2.			
3.			

HARVEST DATES	VARIETY	EXPECTED	ACTUAL
1.			
2.			
3.			

SATISFIED WITH VARIETY, AMOUNT?

1. ______
2. ______
3. ______

NOTES ______

19	VARIETY	DATE PLANTED	AMOUNT PLANTED (ROW LENGTH)
1.			
2.			
3.			

HARVEST DATES	VARIETY	EXPECTED	ACTUAL
1.			
2.			
3.			

SATISFIED WITH VARIETY, AMOUNT?

1. ______
2. ______
3. ______

NOTES ______

19	VARIETY	DATE PLANTED	AMOUNT PLANTED (ROW LENGTH)
1.			
2.			
3.			

HARVEST DATES	VARIETY	EXPECTED	ACTUAL
1.			
2.			
3.			

SATISFIED WITH VARIETY, AMOUNT?

1. ______
2. ______
3. ______

NOTES ______

CRESS: While this name is used loosely to apply to several members of the mustard family, to the gardener this is *Lepidium sativum,* also known as **GARDEN CRESS** and pepper grass, an early spring vegetable, an annual used in salads and easy and quick to grow. Does best in rich soil.

PLANTING: When soil can be worked, seed thickly in rows a foot apart, cover thinly, and stand back and watch it grow. The quickest crop in the garden, cress can be cut for eating in 10 days. Since cress quickly passes its peak, successive plantings should be made weekly until hot weather, when it becomes too hot-tasting. Thin plants to three inches apart. Can be grown indoors in pots.

CULTIVATION: There's hardly time for more than a little weeding.

HARVESTING: If cutting is restrained, several cuttings may be made from each plant.

VARIETIES: *Curlycress* (10 days to first cutting. Pungent flavor).

WATER CRESS *(Nasturtium officinale)* is a perennial bog plant grown along shallow brooks. Can be seeded there, or transplanted to shady, moist location. If good location is found, it will spread into a deep bed. Can be harvested in spring, fall. Good in salads and dainty sandwiches.

19	VARIETY	DATE PLANTED	AMOUNT PLANTED (ROW LENGTH)
1.			
2.			
3.			

HARVEST DATES	VARIETY	EXPECTED	ACTUAL
1.			
2.			
3.			

SATISFIED WITH VARIETY, AMOUNT?
1.
2.
3.

NOTES

19	VARIETY	DATE PLANTED	AMOUNT PLANTED (ROW LENGTH)
1.			
2.			
3.			

HARVEST DATES	VARIETY	EXPECTED	ACTUAL
1.			
2.			
3.			

SATISFIED WITH VARIETY, AMOUNT?
1.
2.
3.

NOTES

19	VARIETY	DATE PLANTED	AMOUNT PLANTED (ROW LENGTH)
1.			
2.			
3.			

HARVEST DATES	VARIETY	EXPECTED	ACTUAL
1.			
2.			
3.			

SATISFIED WITH VARIETY, AMOUNT?
1.
2.
3.

NOTES

CUCUMBER *(Cucumis sativus)* Warm weather annual vine crop grows throughout United States. Fertile loam should be improved with well-rotted manure or compost. If space conservation is essential, cucumbers may be grown along a fence. Quarter-ounce of seed for 50 foot row of hills set 4 feet apart will yield 50 pounds of cucumbers.

PLANTING: At least a week after last frost, in prepared hill sites, four-five feet apart in each direction, plant eight seeds half-inch deep. When plants are four inches tall, thin to four healthiest plants by pinching out others in hill. If grown along fence, seeds should be a foot apart, on alternate sides of fence. Can be started indoors four weeks in advance, in pressed peat pots. Plant two seeds in each pot. Pinch off weaker one when plants reach two inches tall.

CULTIVATION: Mulch heavily, allowing vines to grow over mulch, and water during dry periods. Cultivate lightly and frequently at first. Many methods are used to provide both nutrients and water these plants require. One is to punch holes in lower sides of large tin can, such as a juice can, fill it with compost or rotted manure, bury it in center of cucumber hill, then water through it daily.

HARVESTING: Cucumbers begin producing six to seven weeks after planting. Vines will produce until frost as long as cucumbers are picked before they reach yellow-ripe maturity, so keep them picked, even if they are not needed immediately. Early staminate or male blossoms appear in clusters first, and do not produce cucumbers. Small cucumbers appear below pistillate, or female blossoms. Pick slicing cucumbers when 6-8 inches long, pickling cucumbers when three inches or less.

ENEMIES: Cucumber beetles (striped and 12-spotted) will eat young plants, dine on leaves and stems of larger plants. May be repelled by radishes, nasturtiums or marigolds planted near hills. Hotcaps or cheesecloth on frames over each plant will protect young plants. Fungus diseases such as downy mildew can be avoided by rotation of crops, control of insects and selection of resistant seeds.

VARIETIES: The varieties include slicing and pickling cucumbers. *Marketer* (65 days will produce crisp, flavorful 8-inch slicing cucumbers). *Straight Eight* (58 days. Slicing. Does well in North). *Spartan Valour* (58 days. Slicing. Very slim and dark). *Wisconsin SMR 18* (54 days. Pickling. Good yield. Scab and mosaic disease resistant).

19	VARIETY	DATE PLANTED	AMOUNT PLANTED (ROW LENGTH)
1.			
2.			
3.			

HARVEST DATES	VARIETY	EXPECTED	ACTUAL
1.			
2.			
3.			

SATISFIED WITH VARIETY, AMOUNT?

1. __________
2. __________
3. __________

NOTES __________

19	VARIETY	DATE PLANTED	AMOUNT PLANTED (ROW LENGTH)
1.			
2.			
3.			

HARVEST DATES	VARIETY	EXPECTED	ACTUAL
1.			
2.			
3.			

SATISFIED WITH VARIETY, AMOUNT?

1. __________
2. __________
3. __________

NOTES __________

19	VARIETY	DATE PLANTED	AMOUNT PLANTED (ROW LENGTH)
1.			
2.			
3.			

HARVEST DATES	VARIETY	EXPECTED	ACTUAL
1.			
2.			
3.			

SATISFIED WITH VARIETY, AMOUNT?

1. __________
2. __________
3. __________

NOTES __________

DILL *(Anethum graveolens)* Raise a small amount of this hardy annual if you plan to pickle cucumbers, or if you like a refreshing change of taste in some salads and soups. Easily grown throughout United States. Packet enough for any family needs.

PLANTING: After last frost, sow seed sparingly quarter-inch deep, and thin to plants 12-15 inches apart, since plants will reach maturity more quickly and produce more seeds if not crowded. If more than one row, keep rows three feet apart. Grows about three feet high. Succession plantings recommended for those who add this to their salads.

CULTIVATION: Keep weeded. Dill grows on a fragile, hollow stem, and to prevent it from toppling over, it should be staked when 18 inches high.

HARVESTING: Cut seed heads with short stem in mid-summer, using care to avoid scattering of seeds (and thus sowing next year's crops where it may not be wanted). Dry in shaded area, clean out chaff, store seeds. Fresh and dried leaves are also called for in some recipes. Many pickle recipes call for sprigs of fresh dill flowers.

19 VARIETY	DATE PLANTED	AMOUNT PLANTED (ROW LENGTH)
1.		
2.		
3.		

HARVEST DATES VARIETY	EXPECTED	ACTUAL
1.		
2.		
3.		

SATISFIED WITH VARIETY, AMOUNT?

1.		
2.		
3.		

NOTES

19 VARIETY	DATE PLANTED	AMOUNT PLANTED (ROW LENGTH)
1.		
2.		
3.		

HARVEST DATES VARIETY	EXPECTED	ACTUAL
1.		
2.		
3.		

SATISFIED WITH VARIETY, AMOUNT?

1.		
2.		
3.		

NOTES

19 VARIETY	DATE PLANTED	AMOUNT PLANTED (ROW LENGTH)
1.		
2.		
3.		

HARVEST DATES VARIETY	EXPECTED	ACTUAL
1.		
2.		
3.		

SATISFIED WITH VARIETY, AMOUNT?

1.		
2.		
3.		

NOTES

EGGPLANT *(Solanum melongena)* This fussy plant is worth growing if only for the beauty of its fruit. A delight for the gourmet, eggplant is very sensitive to the weather, but this should not deter the gardener. Needs rich soil, with compost or rotted manure added. A good experimental crop for gardener who has never tried it. Packet of seeds should produce 50 plants, double the number needed for a 50-foot row, and too many for the average family. So save half of seeds for following year.

PLANTING: Start seeds indoors in flats or 3-inch peat pots, 7-8 weeks in advance of transplanting time, which is week after last spring frost, and when soil is warm. Set seeds quarter-inch deep. Set plants out 30 inches apart in rows three feet apart. Soak pots night before transplanting, and shade plants for a day or two afterward.

CULTIVATION: To get a crop, eggplants must be kept warm, moist and fed from the moment of planting the seed. The growth pattern should not be interrupted by lack of moisture or by cold. Keep weeds out of row, sidedress with compost, and mulch well, after plants have gotten a start in warm soil.

HARVESTING: Admiration of the beauty of the fruit should not delay harvesting. When fruit is large and shining, cut it from the plant. If fruits are left until they lose their gloss, the taste will suffer and the plant will stop producing.

ENEMIES: Once provided a good start, eggplants are relatively hardy. Cutworms can be discouraged with paper collars around stems of tiny plants. Use rotenone for flea beetles, Colorado potato beetles and, in the South, the tortoise beetle. To avoid bacterial wilt, avoid planting where potatoes, tomatoes or eggplants have grown in the past three years.

VARIETIES: *Black Beauty* (73 days from transplant to first mature fruit. Good producer of heavy fruit).

19 VARIETY	DATE PLANTED	AMOUNT PLANTED (ROW LENGTH)
1.		
2.		
3.		

HARVEST DATES VARIETY	EXPECTED	ACTUAL
1.		
2.		
3.		

SATISFIED WITH VARIETY, AMOUNT?

1.
2.
3.

NOTES

19 VARIETY	DATE PLANTED	AMOUNT PLANTED (ROW LENGTH)
1.		
2.		
3.		

HARVEST DATES VARIETY	EXPECTED	ACTUAL
1.		
2.		
3.		

SATISFIED WITH VARIETY, AMOUNT?

1.
2.
3.

NOTES

19 VARIETY	DATE PLANTED	AMOUNT PLANTED (ROW LENGTH)
1.		
2.		
3.		

HARVEST DATES VARIETY	EXPECTED	ACTUAL
1.		
2.		
3.		

SATISFIED WITH VARIETY, AMOUNT?

1.
2.
3.

NOTES

ENDIVE *(Cichorium endivia)* a salad plant, sharper in flavor than lettuce. Can be grown throughout United States in most soils, although rich loam is best, with compost or rotted manure raked into row before planting. In South this is a winter crop. In North it can be grown throughout summer. Quarter to a half-ounce of seed for a 50-foot row will produce 50 heads.

PLANTING: As soon as ground can be worked, sow seeds sparsely, cover with thin (¼-½ inch) layer of sifted soil or sifted compost, in rows a foot apart. Thin plants to stand foot apart. Can be started indoors. If so, set transplants slightly deeper outside than they were growing, and shade for a day. Best when sown later, indoors or outdoors, for fall crop. Good crop to follow early lettuce. Will stand frost.

CULTIVATION: Aim is to produce relatively bland endive, so growth must be continuous and rapid or it will become overly pungent. Needs good soil, adequate moisture, ample room. Endive is also blanched to avoid pungency. When half-grown and heads are formed, outer leaves should be drawn around heads, tied with string or held with a rubber band.

HARVESTING: Check heads two weeks after tying to see whether inner leaves are white and ready to eat. Discard outer leaves. If abundant fall crop is raised, dig up entire plant after first frost, keeping ball of earth around the shallow roots. This can be placed in a cool, dark cellar, kept slightly moist, and it will be blanched and last for several months.

VARIETIES: *Broad-leaved Batavian* (90 days to harvesting. Buttery-textured hearts and smooth leaves. Hardy). *Green Curled* (90 days. Finely cut leaves. Blanches to creamy white).

19 VARIETY	DATE PLANTED	AMOUNT PLANTED (ROW LENGTH)
1.		
2.		
3.		

HARVEST DATES VARIETY	EXPECTED	ACTUAL
1.		
2.		
3.		

SATISFIED WITH VARIETY, AMOUNT?

1. ______
2. ______
3. ______

NOTES ______

19 VARIETY	DATE PLANTED	AMOUNT PLANTED (ROW LENGTH)
1.		
2.		
3.		

HARVEST DATES VARIETY	EXPECTED	ACTUAL
1.		
2.		
3.		

SATISFIED WITH VARIETY, AMOUNT?

1. ______
2. ______
3. ______

NOTES ______

19 VARIETY	DATE PLANTED	AMOUNT PLANTED (ROW LENGTH)
1.		
2.		
3.		

HARVEST DATES VARIETY	EXPECTED	ACTUAL
1.		
2.		
3.		

SATISFIED WITH VARIETY, AMOUNT?

1. ______
2. ______
3. ______

NOTES ______

GARLIC *(Allium sativum)* Pungent member of onion family. A perennial that is harvested as an annual, and often is interplanted with cabbages, lettuce and peas to repel insects. Grows one-two feet high. Does best in mild climate, in rich, sandy soil. Pound and one-half of cloves for 50-foot row will yield about 12 pounds of garlic bulbs.

PLANTING: Divide bulbs into cloves, and, as soon as ground can be worked, plant cloves one inch deep, 3-6 inches apart, in rows 12-18 inches apart.

CULTIVATION: Keep weed-free and mulched. Very shallow-rooted, so cultivate cautiously.

HARVESTING: If garlic is in rich soil, and tops do not dry and fall over at end of season, bend them over to mature the bulbs. Pull plants, stack them with tops on top to dry. Then clean them, trim roots close to base. They may be braided, for storage, into picturesque strings, or tied in bundles.

ENEMIES: Same as onion. An onion maggot, the bad-breathed larva of a grey fly, eats into bulb, and will cause it to rot. Burn plants if infested. Scattered planting helps to avoid this problem.

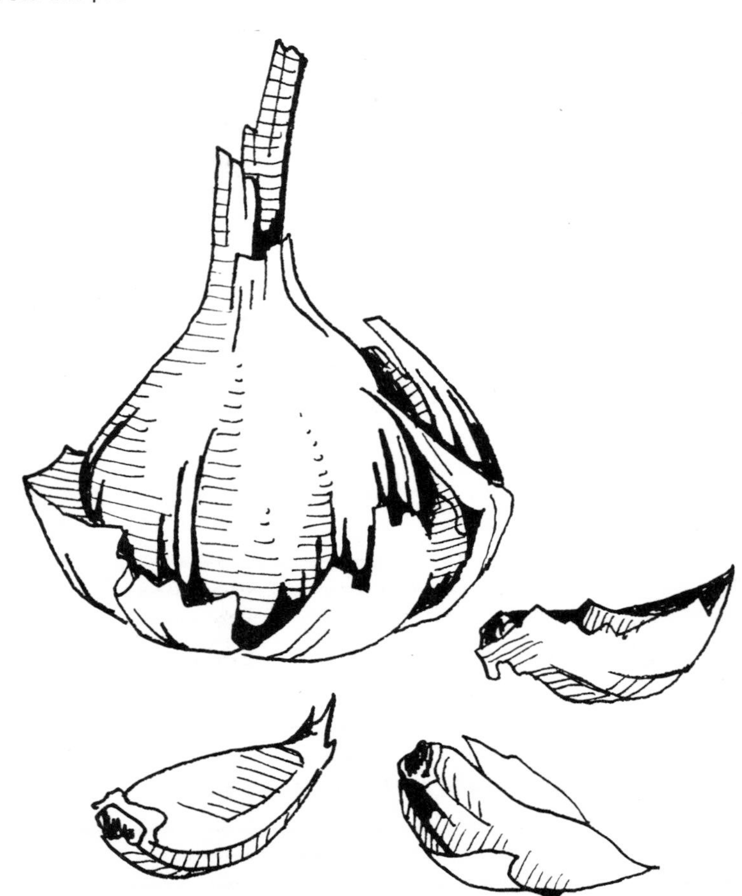

19	VARIETY	DATE PLANTED	AMOUNT PLANTED (ROW LENGTH)
1.			
2.			
3.			

HARVEST DATES	VARIETY	EXPECTED	ACTUAL
1.			
2.			
3.			

SATISFIED WITH VARIETY, AMOUNT?

1. ______
2. ______
3. ______

NOTES ______

19	VARIETY	DATE PLANTED	AMOUNT PLANTED (ROW LENGTH)
1.			
2.			
3.			

HARVEST DATES	VARIETY	EXPECTED	ACTUAL
1.			
2.			
3.			

SATISFIED WITH VARIETY, AMOUNT?

1. ______
2. ______
3. ______

NOTES ______

19	VARIETY	DATE PLANTED	AMOUNT PLANTED (ROW LENGTH)
1.			
2.			
3.			

HARVEST DATES	VARIETY	EXPECTED	ACTUAL
1.			
2.			
3.			

SATISFIED WITH VARIETY, AMOUNT?

1. ______
2. ______
3. ______

NOTES ______

HORSERADISH *(Radicula armoracia)* Perennial raised in temperate regions of the United States where soil freezes in winter. Grown for its thick, white roots which are ground and used as condiment. Prefers rich, deep soil, deeply prepared. Only a few plants needed to meet the needs of a family. Horseradish grows three feet tall, and root system goes as far as 10 feet into ground. Early leaves may be eaten as greens, cooked much like turnip greens.

PLANTING: Propagated with crown of mature plant, or root cuttings, 6-8 inches long and ¼-inch thick. Dig six-inch deep trench, plant roots or place crowns foot apart, making certain roots are planted topside up, and cover with inch or soil.

CULTIVATION: Mulch heavily. Top dress bed with compost each year.

HARVESTING: Can be harvested from late summer until ground is frozen. Dig main roots, leaving side roots to continue growth following season. Common practice is to dig roots as wanted. They should be cleaned, grated into white wine vinegar, then sealed into container. It will gradually lose its snap, so it is best to make it as needed.

ENEMIES: Rotenone will discourage any flea beetles that chance upon this hardy plant.

19	VARIETY	DATE PLANTED	AMOUNT PLANTED (ROW LENGTH)
1.			
2.			
3.			
HARVEST DATES	**VARIETY**	**EXPECTED**	**ACTUAL**
1.			
2.			
3.			
SATISFIED WITH VARIETY, AMOUNT?			
1.			
2.			
3.			

NOTES ______________________________

19	VARIETY	DATE PLANTED	AMOUNT PLANTED (ROW LENGTH)
1.			
2.			
3.			
HARVEST DATES	**VARIETY**	**EXPECTED**	**ACTUAL**
1.			
2.			
3.			
SATISFIED WITH VARIETY, AMOUNT?			
1.			
2.			
3.			

NOTES ______________________________

19	VARIETY	DATE PLANTED	AMOUNT PLANTED (ROW LENGTH)
1.			
2.			
3.			
HARVEST DATES	**VARIETY**	**EXPECTED**	**ACTUAL**
1.			
2.			
3.			
SATISFIED WITH VARIETY, AMOUNT?			
1.			
2.			
3.			

NOTES ______________________________

KALE *(Brassica oleracea acephala)* A hardy member of the cabbage family grown for its large, curled leaves, which are used as greens. Thrives in cool weather. Loam should be deeply prepared, with compost and limestone added. Eighth of an ounce of seed in 50-foot row will yield 30 plants.

PLANTING: Can be planted in early spring, or follow non-cabbage family crops that mature by midsummer. In areas south of Pennsylvania, plants may be left in ground through winter. Sow seeds ½-inch deep, sow sparsely and thin young plants to stand 16 inches apart.

CULTIVATION: Best kale results if plants have plenty of nutrients and water, so that rapid growth is possible. Mulch heavily.

HARVESTING: In South, kale will overwinter and can be harvested in spring. In North, gardeners can cover kale with hay or straw, then harvest it during early winter. While outer leaves only may be harvested as they develop, usual method is to cut entire plant, before it becomes stringy and tough. Boil it, like spinach. Some like new leaves in salads.

ENEMIES: Flea beetles usually are not a serious threat when weeds are eliminated.

VARIETIES: *Vates* (60 days to harvesting. Attractive plant with finely curled bluish-green leaves). *Blue Curled Scotch* (55 days. Low, compact plants).

19 VARIETY	DATE PLANTED	AMOUNT PLANTED (ROW LENGTH)
1.		
2.		
3.		

HARVEST DATES VARIETY	EXPECTED	ACTUAL
1.		
2.		
3.		

SATISFIED WITH VARIETY, AMOUNT?

1.
2.
3.

NOTES

19 VARIETY	DATE PLANTED	AMOUNT PLANTED (ROW LENGTH)
1.		
2.		
3.		

HARVEST DATES VARIETY	EXPECTED	ACTUAL
1.		
2.		
3.		

SATISFIED WITH VARIETY, AMOUNT?

1.
2.
3.

NOTES

19 VARIETY	DATE PLANTED	AMOUNT PLANTED (ROW LENGTH)
1.		
2.		
3.		

HARVEST DATES VARIETY	EXPECTED	ACTUAL
1.		
2.		
3.		

SATISFIED WITH VARIETY, AMOUNT?

1.
2.
3.

NOTES

KOHLRABI *(Brassica oleracea caulorapa)* Easily-grown and curious member of the cabbage family. Gardeners who haven't grown this should try it, if only to see and taste it. It is grown for its swollen stem, which resembles an above-ground turnip. This is a cool weather plant. Should have rich, well-drained soil, with lime raked in. Half-ounce of seed in 50-foot row will yield 30 pounds.

PLANTING: Can be started indoors, six weeks before planting date, which is as soon as ground can be worked. It is usually seeded directly at that time, and succession of small plantings is best. Plant seeds half-inch deep, four inches apart, in rows 15 inches apart.

CULTIVATION: Keep free of weeds, well watered and heavily fed. Mulching will help produce a good crop.

HARVESTING: Pick when swollen stem reaches two inches in diameter, or about the size of a golf ball. When larger, kohlrabi becomes tough. In fall, before heavy freeze, harvest with roots, store in cold on bed of straw and covered with straw. Kohlrabi can be sliced raw into salads, or steamed or boiled in its skin.

ENEMIES: Has the same enemies as cabbage, but most are discouraged by good cultivation.

VARIETIES: *Early White Vienna* (55 days to harvesting. Mild flavor. Creamy white flesh). *Early Purple Vienna* (60 days. Purple bulbs, greenish white flesh. These bulbs may be grown slightly larger than Early Whites before eating).

19	VARIETY	DATE PLANTED	AMOUNT PLANTED (ROW LENGTH)
1.			
2.			
3.			

HARVEST DATES	VARIETY	EXPECTED	ACTUAL
1.			
2.			
3.			

SATISFIED WITH VARIETY, AMOUNT?

1.
2.
3.

NOTES

19	VARIETY	DATE PLANTED	AMOUNT PLANTED (ROW LENGTH)
1.			
2.			
3.			

HARVEST DATES	VARIETY	EXPECTED	ACTUAL
1.			
2.			
3.			

SATISFIED WITH VARIETY, AMOUNT?

1.
2.
3.

NOTES

19	VARIETY	DATE PLANTED	AMOUNT PLANTED (ROW LENGTH)
1.			
2.			
3.			

HARVEST DATES	VARIETY	EXPECTED	ACTUAL
1.			
2.			
3.			

SATISFIED WITH VARIETY, AMOUNT?

1.
2.
3.

NOTES

LEEK *(Allium porrum)* A sweet, bland member of the onion family, well worth growing because of its many uses, both raw and cooked. Can be grown throughout the United States, in a variety of soils, but does best in temperate climate and soil rich in nitrogen. Leeks form thick, fleshy cylinders that resemble large green onions. A half-ounce of seed in a 50-foot row should yield 100 plants.

PLANTING: Sow seed half-inch deep in flats indoors eight weeks before last frost. When transplanting to garden, as they reach about eight inches high, cut back half of grass-like growth. In well-drained area, dig trench six inches deep and four inches wide, with rows 18 inches apart. Put in an inch-deep layer of compost. Transplant six inches apart in bottom of trench.

CULTIVATION: Gradually fill in trench as leeks grow, to blanch them and thus make them more tender. When they have reached full growth, entire stem should be banked, for blanching.

HARVESTING: Leeks can be picked and eaten before reaching maturity. For late fall use, leeks may be left in ground until after heavy frost, then dug, packed closely and stored in unheated building. Late-started crop can be overwintered by mulching heavily with hay or straw, and they will produce a delicious spring crop. Leeks are liked by cooks, since they add a delicate flavor, fresh in salads, or cooked in soups.

ENEMIES: Leeks have few enemies and are easily grown. If rot is detected, onion maggot, the larva of a small, grey fly, may be responsible. Destroy those plants.

VARIETIES: *Broad London* (130 days to maturity, but are edible before this time).

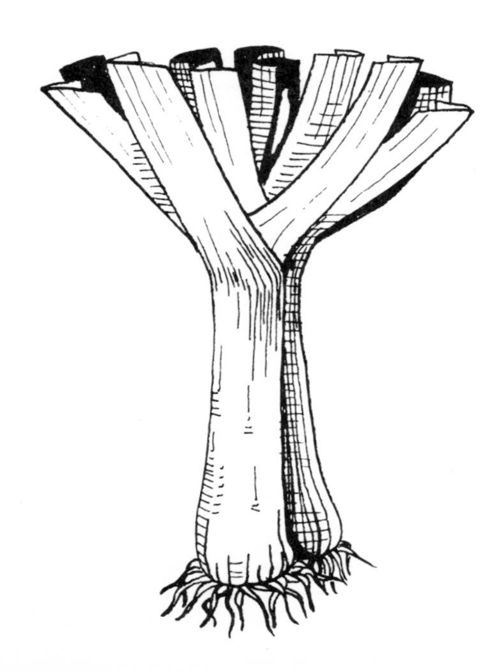

19 VARIETY | DATE PLANTED | AMOUNT PLANTED (ROW LENGTH)

1. ____________________ ________ ________
2. ____________________ ________ ________
3. ____________________ ________ ________

HARVEST DATES VARIETY | EXPECTED | ACTUAL

1. ____________________ ________ ________
2. ____________________ ________ ________
3. ____________________ ________ ________

SATISFIED WITH VARIETY, AMOUNT?

1. ____________________ ________ ________
2. ____________________ ________ ________
3. ____________________ ________ ________

NOTES ____________________

19 VARIETY | DATE PLANTED | AMOUNT PLANTED (ROW LENGTH)

1. ____________________ ________ ________
2. ____________________ ________ ________
3. ____________________ ________ ________

HARVEST DATES VARIETY | EXPECTED | ACTUAL

1. ____________________ ________ ________
2. ____________________ ________ ________
3. ____________________ ________ ________

SATISFIED WITH VARIETY, AMOUNT?

1. ____________________ ________ ________
2. ____________________ ________ ________
3. ____________________ ________ ________

NOTES ____________________

19 VARIETY | DATE PLANTED | AMOUNT PLANTED (ROW LENGTH)

1. ____________________ ________ ________
2. ____________________ ________ ________
3. ____________________ ________ ________

HARVEST DATES VARIETY | EXPECTED | ACTUAL

1. ____________________ ________ ________
2. ____________________ ________ ________
3. ____________________ ________ ________

SATISFIED WITH VARIETY, AMOUNT?

1. ____________________ ________ ________
2. ____________________ ________ ________
3. ____________________ ________ ________

NOTES ____________________

LETTUCE, LOOSE-LEAF: *(Lactuca sativa)* Make room in your garden for this lettuce, no matter how small your plot is. It's easy to grow and there is a wide variety, each with its own merits. Grown throughout United States. Lettuce plants should be grown quickly, and not crowded. Dig compost or well-rotted manure into soil. Thrives in cool weather, will stand considerable frost, and is very sensitive to heat. Will grow in mid-summer only in far North. An eighth of an ounce of seed in 50-foot row will yield 30 pounds.

PLANTING: To get lettuce from garden as early as possible, and thus avoid buying the expensive, inferior varieties found in stores, plant indoors six weeks before last spring frost. When ground can be worked, transplant this, and at the same time start more from seed. Transplants should be 8-10 inches apart. Sow seeds sparingly quarter-inch deep, and gradually thin to 8-10 inches apart, using thinnings for salads.

CULTIVATION: Lettuce almost takes care of itself. Sift light mulch around young plants to deter growth of weeds, gradually build up layer of mulch to provide cool, moist conditions this crop likes. Water liberally if season is dry.

HARVESTING: Lettuce is good at all stages to maturity, but should be harvested before it shoots to seed and turns bitter. It is crispest in the morning. Should be cut at root level, washed and stored in refrigerator crisper until needed.

ENEMIES: Rot at base of plants usually due to crowding. Rotation urged to avoid fungus and bacterial diseases. Collars around transplants will thwart cutworms. Slugs dislike scattering of wood ashes or lime, and will give up their lives for a short beer in a saucer.

VARIETIES: *Salad Bowl* (45 days to maturity. Crisp and tender. Almost foolproof for a good crop). *Oak Leaf* (40 days. Pick outer leaves only and it will keep producing. One of the more heat-resistent of leaf lettuces).

19 VARIETY	DATE PLANTED	AMOUNT PLANTED (ROW LENGTH)
1.		
2.		
3.		

HARVEST DATES VARIETY	EXPECTED	ACTUAL
1.		
2.		
3.		

SATISFIED WITH VARIETY, AMOUNT?

1. ____
2. ____
3. ____

NOTES ____

19 VARIETY	DATE PLANTED	AMOUNT PLANTED (ROW LENGTH)
1.		
2.		
3.		

HARVEST DATES VARIETY	EXPECTED	ACTUAL
1.		
2.		
3.		

SATISFIED WITH VARIETY, AMOUNT?

1. ____
2. ____
3. ____

NOTES ____

19 VARIETY	DATE PLANTED	AMOUNT PLANTED (ROW LENGTH)
1.		
2.		
3.		

HARVEST DATES VARIETY	EXPECTED	ACTUAL
1.		
2.		
3.		

SATISFIED WITH VARIETY, AMOUNT?

1. ____
2. ____
3. ____

NOTES ____

LETTUCE, HEAD *(Lactuca sativa)* Try both butter head and iceberg or crisp head varieties. Head lettuce is more difficult to grow than loose leaf, and is more sensitive to heat. Prepare rows by raking in compost or well-rotted manure. Grow best in North in early spring or fall, in South in fall, winter and spring. When selecting varieties, ask Extension Agents or proficient gardeners for advice on what grows best in area. Eighth of an ounce of seed in 50-foot row will yield 50 heads.

PLANTING: Start head lettuce in flats indoors, six weeks before date of last frost. Transplant when ground can be worked, spacing plants a foot apart in rows 18-24 inches apart. Adjacent plants should never touch.

CULTIVATION: Mulch with compost to keep out weeds. Keep well watered. If weather is hot before heads are formed, provide shade. This can be done with a canopy of netting or a double thickness of cheesecloth suspended on stakes two feet above crop, and removable for rains or sprinkling.

HARVESTING: Harvesting can start before heads are filled. Best to harvest in morning, when lettuce is crispest.

ENEMIES: Crowded conditions may lead to rot. Rotation urged to avoid fungus and bacterial diseases. Collars around transplants will thwart cutworms. Slugs dislike scattering of wood ashes or lime, and will be drawn to beer in a saucer.

VARIETIES: *Butter Crunch* (75 days to mature head. A superior butter head, tasty, crisp and slow to bolt). *Dark Green Boston* (80 days. Delicious butter head). *Great Lakes* (90 days. Heavy iceberg and good quality. Stands up well in heat).

19	VARIETY	DATE PLANTED	AMOUNT PLANTED (ROW LENGTH)
1.			
2.			
3.			

HARVEST DATES	VARIETY	EXPECTED	ACTUAL
1.			
2.			
3.			

SATISFIED WITH VARIETY, AMOUNT?

1.
2.
3.

NOTES

19	VARIETY	DATE PLANTED	AMOUNT PLANTED (ROW LENGTH)
1.			
2.			
3.			

HARVEST DATES	VARIETY	EXPECTED	ACTUAL
1.			
2.			
3.			

SATISFIED WITH VARIETY, AMOUNT?

1.
2.
3.

NOTES

19	VARIETY	DATE PLANTED	AMOUNT PLANTED (ROW LENGTH)
1.			
2.			
3.			

HARVEST DATES	VARIETY	EXPECTED	ACTUAL
1.			
2.			
3.			

SATISFIED WITH VARIETY, AMOUNT?

1.
2.
3.

NOTES

MUSKMELON, including cantaloupe *(Cucumis melo)* In United States most muskmelons are referred to incorrectly as cantaloupes, which are one of several varieties of muskmelons. All require warm, sandy loam, with long season of warmth and sunlight. Persons hoping to raise these should find varieties raised with success in their areas before purchasing seeds. Most melons require a growing season above 55° at night and above 80° in the daytime. Even if started indoors, they will not mature properly if temperatures dip below those levels at end of growing season. Require feeding early in season, using compost or well-rotted manure. Fifty-foot row should yield 30 melons.

PLANTING: In northern areas, sow seeds indoors or in hotbed a month before temperatures reach desired 55° night, 80° day temperatures. Sow seeds or transplants in garden when those temperatures are reached, placing two transplants or 6-8 seeds in each hill, four feet apart each way. Hills should be prepared with compost or well-rotted manure dug in, a spadeful or more per hill. If seeds are planted, cut off all but best two in each hill when seedlings are about four inches high.

CULTIVATION: Melons are shallow rooted, so cultivate carefully, or better, mulch heavily. Avoid moving vines. Constant supply of moisture a must. Remove melons that set late in season, to improve size and quality of others.

HARVESTING: Cantaloupes are ready to be eaten when they are at "slip" stage, and slight pressure on vine will cause melon to slip off. Other melons are judged by scent or color.

ENEMIES: Starting melons indoors lessens chances of trouble from striped cucumber beetle, which attacks seedlings and spreads fusarium wilt. Beetles can be hand picked. Hotcaps can also be used for protection from beetles. Downy and powdery mildew are worse in wet weather. Varieties tolerant to both mildew and wilt are available.

VARIETIES: *Hearts of Gold* (90 days to maturity. Orange flesh, extremely sweet). *Hale's Best* (85 days. Salmon flesh). Selection is a matter of learning what grows best in area, and experimenting.

19 VARIETY	DATE PLANTED	AMOUNT PLANTED (ROW LENGTH)
1.		
2.		
3.		

HARVEST DATES VARIETY	EXPECTED	ACTUAL
1.		
2.		
3.		

SATISFIED WITH VARIETY, AMOUNT?

1.
2.
3.

NOTES

19 VARIETY	DATE PLANTED	AMOUNT PLANTED (ROW LENGTH)
1.		
2.		
3.		

HARVEST DATES VARIETY	EXPECTED	ACTUAL
1.		
2.		
3.		

SATISFIED WITH VARIETY, AMOUNT?

1.
2.
3.

NOTES

19 VARIETY	DATE PLANTED	AMOUNT PLANTED (ROW LENGTH)
1.		
2.		
3.		

HARVEST DATES VARIETY	EXPECTED	ACTUAL
1.		
2.		
3.		

SATISFIED WITH VARIETY, AMOUNT?

1.
2.
3.

NOTES

MUSTARD GREENS *(Brassica juncea)* Grown primarily in the South for cooked mustard greens and for salads. Enthusiasm for this vegetable outside that area is held well in check, although they can be grown anywhere in the United States. Sandy loam preferred. A quarter-ounce of seed for a 50-foot row, with yield depending on size it is permitted to grow, and the number of cuttings.

PLANTING: As soon as ground can be worked, sow seed sparsely, half-inch deep in rows 12 inches apart. Thin plants to six inches apart. Successive plantings can be made until a month before heat of summer.

CULTIVATION: Mulch with compost.

HARVESTING: These green are rich in vitamins and minerals. Cut leaves with shears, and not too close, or continuing yield will be halted. For salads, cut at four inches. Let it grow to six inches for cooking greens.

VARIETIES: *Florida Broad Leaf* (43 days. Easy to prepare as greens, because of broad, smooth leaves). *Tendergreen* (35 days. More rapid growing. Flavor is much like spinach).

19	VARIETY	DATE PLANTED	AMOUNT PLANTED (ROW LENGTH)
1.			
2.			
3.			

HARVEST DATES	VARIETY	EXPECTED	ACTUAL
1.			
2.			
3.			

SATISFIED WITH VARIETY, AMOUNT?
1.
2.
3.

NOTES

19	VARIETY	DATE PLANTED	AMOUNT PLANTED (ROW LENGTH)
1.			
2.			
3.			

HARVEST DATES	VARIETY	EXPECTED	ACTUAL
1.			
2.			
3.			

SATISFIED WITH VARIETY, AMOUNT?
1.
2.
3.

NOTES

19	VARIETY	DATE PLANTED	AMOUNT PLANTED (ROW LENGTH)
1.			
2.			
3.			

HARVEST DATES	VARIETY	EXPECTED	ACTUAL
1.			
2.			
3.			

SATISFIED WITH VARIETY, AMOUNT?
1.
2.
3.

NOTES

NEW ZEALAND SPINACH: *(Tetragonia expansa)* Not a true spinach, but often grown to provide greens in period between spring and fall, when spinach does not grow well. More heat-tolerant than spinach, and equally rich in vitamins and minerals. Does not look like spinach but tastes much like it when cooked. Deeply prepared loam is best. Quarter-ounce of seed in 50-foot row will produce 40 pounds.

PLANTING: Soak seed in cold water 24 hours to speed the deliberate pace of its germination. One week after last killing frost, plant very sparsely one inch deep in rows three feet apart, and thin plants to 18-24 inches apart. Some gardeners plant this sprawling annual in hills, three seeds to a hill, then thin each to one plant. Hills are three feet apart in rows four feet apart.

CULTIVATION: Mulch heavily to preserve moisture.

HARVESTING: Break off 3-4 inches of tip and cook like other greens—briefly. Harvesting can continue until after first frosts, which this plant can withstand.

19	VARIETY	DATE PLANTED	AMOUNT PLANTED (ROW LENGTH)
1.			
2.			
3.			

HARVEST DATES	VARIETY	EXPECTED	ACTUAL
1.			
2.			
3.			

SATISFIED WITH VARIETY, AMOUNT?

1. ______
2. ______
3. ______

NOTES ______

19	VARIETY	DATE PLANTED	AMOUNT PLANTED (ROW LENGTH)
1.			
2.			
3.			

HARVEST DATES	VARIETY	EXPECTED	ACTUAL
1.			
2.			
3.			

SATISFIED WITH VARIETY, AMOUNT?

1. ______
2. ______
3. ______

NOTES ______

19	VARIETY	DATE PLANTED	AMOUNT PLANTED (ROW LENGTH)
1.			
2.			
3.			

HARVEST DATES	VARIETY	EXPECTED	ACTUAL
1.			
2.			
3.			

SATISFIED WITH VARIETY, AMOUNT?

1. ______
2. ______
3. ______

NOTES ______

OKRA *(Hibiscus esculentus)* Also called gumbo. Tall (3-5 feet) tropical annual grown for its immature pods which are fried or cooked in stews, soups and meat dishes, mostly in the South. Ounce of seed in 40-foot row will provide 30 pounds of pods every two weeks, triple the amount most families will want.

PLANTING: Week after last spring frost, when soil is warm, sow seeds half-inch deep, three-four seeds to a hill, with hills 18 inches apart, in rows three feet apart. When seedlings are two inches tall, snip off all but strongest one in each hill. Can also be started in peat pots, month in advance, putting two seeds in each pot, and later cutting off the weaker seedling. When night temperatures remain above 50°, plant pots 18 inches apart, in rows three feet apart.

CULTIVATION: Mulch with compost.

HARVESTING: When pods are 2-3 inches long they should be picked. If they are allowed to become mature (7-9 inches), plants will stop producing. Pods follow bloom of maroon-centered pale yellow flowers.

ENEMIES: Hand-pick the green stink bugs and cabbage loopers that may be found in okra.

VARIETIES: **Clemson Spineless* (46 days from planting to first edible pods. Good producer. Four-foot plants). *Dwarf Green Long Pod* (52 days. Plants grow 2-2½ feet high, produce fleshy, dark green pods).

19	VARIETY	DATE PLANTED	AMOUNT PLANTED (ROW LENGTH)
1.			
2.			
3.			

HARVEST DATES	VARIETY	EXPECTED	ACTUAL
1.			
2.			
3.			

SATISFIED WITH VARIETY, AMOUNT?

1.
2.
3.

NOTES

19	VARIETY	DATE PLANTED	AMOUNT PLANTED (ROW LENGTH)
1.			
2.			
3.			

HARVEST DATES	VARIETY	EXPECTED	ACTUAL
1.			
2.			
3.			

SATISFIED WITH VARIETY, AMOUNT?

1.
2.
3.

NOTES

19	VARIETY	DATE PLANTED	AMOUNT PLANTED (ROW LENGTH)
1.			
2.			
3.			

HARVEST DATES	VARIETY	EXPECTED	ACTUAL
1.			
2.			
3.			

SATISFIED WITH VARIETY, AMOUNT?

1.
2.
3.

NOTES

ONIONS *(Allium cepa)* Gardener should try several varieties. Onions produce well in limited space, and rare is the gardener who raises too many. In planning on storage, it should be remembered that the stronger the flavor, the longer the onion will keep. Fertile, moist soil enriched with compost is needed. Grow anywhere in United States. Gardener has three choices: Seeds (quarter-ounce in 50-foot row will produce 25 pounds), plants (300 in 50-foot row will produce 30 pounds) and sets (one pound in 50-foot row will produce 30 pounds). Seeds are cheapest, most difficult to raise but provide the greatest selection of varieties. Seeds should be fresh each year. Plants are very dependable if they can be found. Sets, tiny onions grown the previous year, are easiest to handle but are available in only a few varieties. The quality of the crop is linked closely with the quality and size (they should be about the size of a dime) of the sets.

PLANTING: Seeds should be started indoors 8-10 weeks in advance of transplanting. When ground can be worked, clip green growth of seedlings to three inches, then plant them in garden two inches deep, three inches apart in rows a foot apart. Set plants same way and at same time. If seeds are planted outdoors, when ground can be worked, sow 4 or 5 seeds per inch, one inch deep, and transplant thinnings to three inches apart. If sets are used, press them into ground in trenches 2-3 inches deep, with onions set four inches apart, in rows a foot apart. Do not cover.

CULTIVATION: Mulch and cultivate carefully to control weeds.

HARVESTING: As onion tops mature, break them down, to speed ripening. When tops are yellow and dry, pull up plants, cut off tops inch above bulbs, and spread them in dry, shady place to cure. Use thick-necked bulbs first, as they do not store as well. Onions grown from seed will store best. Store in cool, dry and dark place.

ENEMIES: It is not often that the home gardener is troubled with either pests or disease in his onion rows. Onion maggot, a tiny, white worm-like creature, may attack seedlings, causing them to rot. If they invade larger onions, which are stored, they will cause a rot that will spread to others stored. Destroy onions where rot is detected,to interrupt life cycle of the maggot. In the South, onion thrips (so small they are difficult to see) feed on foliage, leaving white areas. Can be washed off with hose.

VARIETIES: For SETS, *Yellow Ebenezer* (100 days to maturity. Good for spring green onions or as cooking onions in fall). For PLANTS, *Sweet Spanish,* a heavy producer. For SEEDS, *Sweet Spanish* (110 days. Very large and mild. Not a keeper). *Yellow Globe* (102 days. High yield. Good keeper).

SCALLIONS, or bunching onions, are onions picked before they develop bulbs, and eaten raw. These are sowed from early spring to midsummer, outdoors and exactly like other onions, and are ready for eating in about 60 days. Varieties include *Southport White Bunching* (mature early, good for either a summer or fall crop) and *Evergreen Long White Bunching* (can be sown for fall crop or heavily mulched and overwintered for early spring crop).

19	VARIETY	DATE PLANTED	AMOUNT PLANTED (ROW LENGTH)
1.			
2.			
3.			

HARVEST DATES	VARIETY	EXPECTED	ACTUAL
1.			
2.			
3.			

SATISFIED WITH VARIETY, AMOUNT?

1.			
2.			
3.			

NOTES ______

19	VARIETY	DATE PLANTED	AMOUNT PLANTED (ROW LENGTH)
1.			
2.			
3.			

HARVEST DATES	VARIETY	EXPECTED	ACTUAL
1.			
2.			
3.			

SATISFIED WITH VARIETY, AMOUNT?

1.			
2.			
3.			

NOTES ______

19	VARIETY	DATE PLANTED	AMOUNT PLANTED (ROW LENGTH)
1.			
2.			
3.			

HARVEST DATES	VARIETY	EXPECTED	ACTUAL
1.			
2.			
3.			

SATISFIED WITH VARIETY, AMOUNT?

1.			
2.			
3.			

NOTES ______

PARSLEY *(Petroselinum crispum)* Its value in the kitchen is great, the space it takes is small. This biennial herb is cultivated for the foliage it produces. Rich in vitamins A and C, its green leaves and stems decorate as well as flavor potato dishes, sauces and soups. Twelve plants more than enough for a family. Does well in any garden soil, but, like chives, it should be planted as close to the kitchen as possible, since it will be used regularly. Seed should be fresh each year. A packet will sow a 100-foot row.

PLANTING: Seed germinates very slowly, taking up to four weeks. Soaking seed in tepid water for 24 hours will speed this. Hoe shallow trench, fill it with compost or well-rotted manure, sow seed rather thickly, cover it with quarter-inch of compost, firm and water it. When plants finally emerge, thin to 3-6 inches apart, depending on variety. If more than one row, keep them 12-15 inches apart. For convenience, parsley can be grown in pots or window boxes, and will do well.

CULTIVATION: Keep free of weeds. As plants mature, sidedress with compost. In late fall, a few plants may be heavily mulched, and will overwinter. Or in fall, plants may be dug up and potted, thus providing cuttings through winter.

HARVESTING: Clip outer leaves as needed, when 4-6 inches high. Leaves may be picked and dried, crumbled into flakes for use in winter.

VARIETIES: *Extra Curled Dwarf* (85 days. Compact plants. Good for overwintering).

19	VARIETY	DATE PLANTED	AMOUNT PLANTED (ROW LENGTH)
1.			
2.			
3.			

HARVEST DATES	VARIETY	EXPECTED	ACTUAL
1.			
2.			
3.			

SATISFIED WITH VARIETY, AMOUNT?
1.
2.
3.

NOTES

19	VARIETY	DATE PLANTED	AMOUNT PLANTED (ROW LENGTH)
1.			
2.			
3.			

HARVEST DATES	VARIETY	EXPECTED	ACTUAL
1.			
2.			
3.			

SATISFIED WITH VARIETY, AMOUNT?
1.
2.
3.

NOTES

19	VARIETY	DATE PLANTED	AMOUNT PLANTED (ROW LENGTH)
1.			
2.			
3.			

HARVEST DATES	VARIETY	EXPECTED	ACTUAL
1.			
2.			
3.			

SATISFIED WITH VARIETY, AMOUNT?
1.
2.
3.

NOTES

PARSNIP *(Pastinaca sativa)* A biennial most often grown in the North, since heavy frost or freezing is needed to improve flavor of roots. Slow to germinate, equally leisurely in growth. While parsnip is a dish rarely served at functions of state, it deserves a try by every gardener who welcomes a change in diet. Needs light soil, worked deeply and with well-rotted manure or compost added. Use fresh seed each year. Quarter-ounce of seed in 50-foot row will yield 50 pounds of parsnips.

PLANTING: When ground has warmed, and after last frost, sow seeds rather thickly, half inch deep, and toss in a few radish seeds to mark the rows. Cover with fine compost. Moisten well with thin spray, cover with damp burlap, to maintain moisture around the seeds.

CULTIVATION: Plants will send roots down to moist levels, but before plants have reached this stage, they should be dampened regularly. Mulch well as plants emerge.

HARVESTING: May be harvested in fall, or mulched heavily and harvested during the winter, or—and this is usual way—dug up in the spring.

ENEMIES: Parsnips are sometimes bothered by carrot rust fly, the maggot of which eats into tap root of parsnips, celery and carrots. Delay planting a few weeks, or cover young plants with cheesecloth draped on frame. Celery blight is avoided by weeding well.

VARIETIES: **Hollow Crown* (105 days. Broad, tapered 12-inch roots. Heavy yield). *Model* (120 days. Longer, slimmer than Hollow Crown).

19 VARIETY	DATE PLANTED	AMOUNT PLANTED (ROW LENGTH)
1.		
2.		
3.		

HARVEST DATES VARIETY	EXPECTED	ACTUAL
1.		
2.		
3.		

SATISFIED WITH VARIETY, AMOUNT?

1.
2.
3.

NOTES

19 VARIETY	DATE PLANTED	AMOUNT PLANTED (ROW LENGTH)
1.		
2.		
3.		

HARVEST DATES VARIETY	EXPECTED	ACTUAL
1.		
2.		
3.		

SATISFIED WITH VARIETY, AMOUNT?

1.
2.
3.

NOTES

19 VARIETY	DATE PLANTED	AMOUNT PLANTED (ROW LENGTH)
1.		
2.		
3.		

HARVEST DATES VARIETY	EXPECTED	ACTUAL
1.		
2.		
3.		

SATISFIED WITH VARIETY, AMOUNT?

1.
2.
3.

NOTES

PEANUT *(Arachis hypogaea)* Easy to grow in South, with few enemies. A challenge for Northern gardeners, but a challenge more and more are accepting, and they're succeeding in their efforts. Acid, light sandy soil with high organic material content. Requires 4-5 months growing season.

PLANTING: In North, get seed grown in that latitude, plant in sunny, protected location. In South, plant after last frost; in North, about time of last frost date. Hull the nuts, plant them 1-2 inches deep, and place them 3-6 inches apart, in rows 30 inches apart.

CULTIVATION: Plants grow 1-1½ feet high, produce flowers on stems that bend, touch ground, then root themselves into ground. Peanuts then form in clusters underground. When plants are a foot high, hill them, pulling soil up around them, then mulch between rows.

HARVESTING: In South, dig vines before frost, cure the peanuts about two months in open shed. In North, in mid-October dig vines and hang them in attic or some other dry place. Cure peanuts about two months. Roast nuts 20 minutes in oven at 300°.

VARIETIES: *Spanish* (110 days. Dwarf bushes. Heavy bearer). *Jumbo Virginia* (120 days. Larger vines).

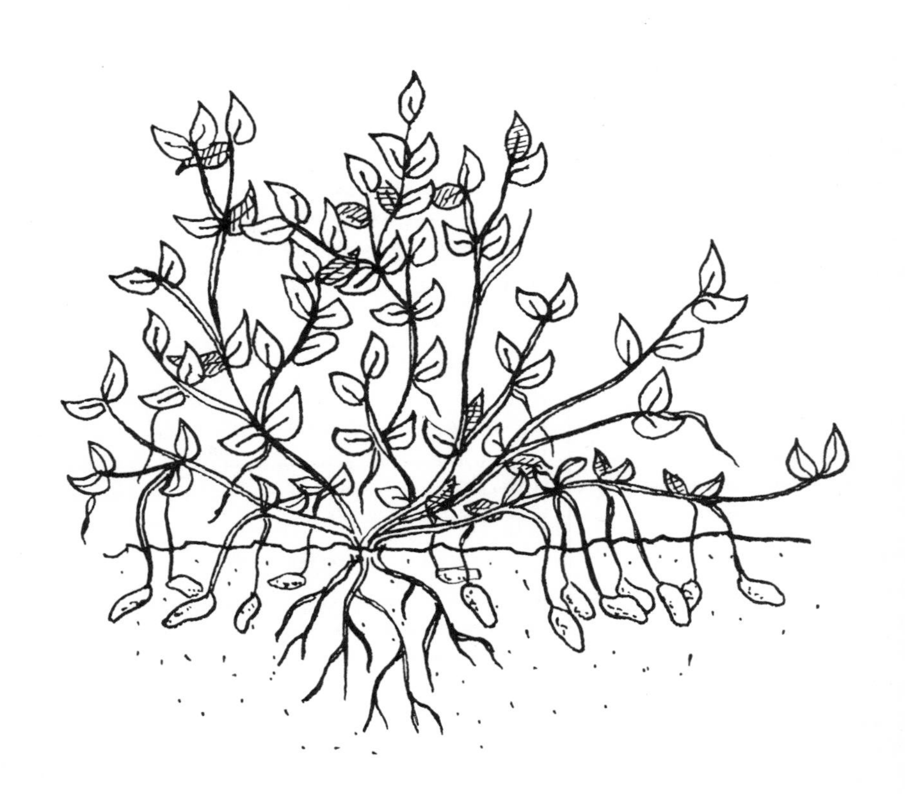

19 VARIETY	DATE PLANTED	AMOUNT PLANTED (ROW LENGTH)
1.		
2.		
3.		

HARVEST DATES VARIETY	EXPECTED	ACTUAL
1.		
2.		
3.		

SATISFIED WITH VARIETY, AMOUNT?

1.
2.
3.

NOTES

19 VARIETY	DATE PLANTED	AMOUNT PLANTED (ROW LENGTH)
1.		
2.		
3.		

HARVEST DATES VARIETY	EXPECTED	ACTUAL
1.		
2.		
3.		

SATISFIED WITH VARIETY, AMOUNT?

1.
2.
3.

NOTES

19 VARIETY	DATE PLANTED	AMOUNT PLANTED (ROW LENGTH)
1.		
2.		
3.		

HARVEST DATES VARIETY	EXPECTED	ACTUAL
1.		
2.		
3.		

SATISFIED WITH VARIETY, AMOUNT?

1.
2.
3.

NOTES

PEAS *(Pisum sativum)* This legume is one of the tastiest reasons for a home garden. Peas are grown throughout the United States, but do best in cool climates such as are found in western Washington, the New England states and states bordering Canada. Peas for planting are smooth (hardier, so can be planted earlier) and wrinkled (later, but worth the wait). The varieties include bush peas, growing 1½-2 feet, easier to grow and take less space, and the tall varieties, which are more prolific and tastier, but with a longer growing season. Sandy loam with ample humus required, plus good supply of phosphorous and potash, but not overly rich in nitrogen. Half-pound of peas in 50-foot row should yield 30 pounds. Difficult to grow too many, for immediate family needs plus freezing.

SOWING: Dust seed with nitrogen inoculant, for better crop plus added nitrogen in soil. As soon as ground can be worked, plant seed one inch deep, spaced two-three inches apart, with rows three feet apart. If bush peas are planted, space between rows can be used for early crop, such as lettuce. Soaking peas before planting recommended only if ground is dry. Instead of successive plantings for longer harvest, plant early and later varieties at the same time. All varieties need some support. For bush peas, heavy mulch can provide this, or, when planting, set in well-branched twigs three feet high. For vine types, use longer twigs and branches, four-five feet high, or four-foot chicken wire well supported. If chicken wire is used, plant double row, with chicken wire between them.

CULTIVATION: Keep weeds out of young plants. Irrigate if spring rain does not provide enough moisture, and be certain there is enough moisture in critical period when pods are filling out. Mulch well.

HARVESTING: Harvest when pods are young and tender and as soon as they are well filled, but before they begin to turn color. Shell and cook as soon after picking as possible. Peas are a delight to freeze, losing but little of their "fresh" flavor.

ENEMIES: If vines are supported, not crowded and not hindered by weeds, peas have few enemies.

VARIETIES: Experiment each year to find varieties that best meet your requirements, recording your successes (and disappointments) each year.

**Little Marvel* (63 days from planting to eating. 18-inch high bushes, wrinkled seed. Does better if supported although it will grow without. Tasty both fresh and frozen). *Progress #9* (60 days. 20-inch bushes, wrinkled seed. Resistant to fusarium wilt. Productive and delicious). **Lincoln* (75 days. This is it for the gourmet who will wait a few days for the best. Wrinkled seed. Heavy crop). And, if you have some extra room, try the EDIBLE POD varieties, such as *Dwarf Gray Sugar* (65 days. Two-foot vines. Sweet and tender. Don't shell. Cook like snap beans).

19	VARIETY	DATE PLANTED	AMOUNT PLANTED (ROW LENGTH)
1.			
2.			
3.			

HARVEST DATES	VARIETY	EXPECTED	ACTUAL
1.			
2.			
3.			

SATISFIED WITH VARIETY, AMOUNT?

1.
2.
3.

NOTES

19	VARIETY	DATE PLANTED	AMOUNT PLANTED (ROW LENGTH)
1.			
2.			
3.			

HARVEST DATES	VARIETY	EXPECTED	ACTUAL
1.			
2.			
3.			

SATISFIED WITH VARIETY, AMOUNT?

1.
2.
3.

NOTES

19	VARIETY	DATE PLANTED	AMOUNT PLANTED (ROW LENGTH)
1.			
2.			
3.			

HARVEST DATES	VARIETY	EXPECTED	ACTUAL
1.			
2.			
3.			

SATISFIED WITH VARIETY, AMOUNT?

1.
2.
3.

NOTES

PEPPERS *(Capsicum)* Including the hot varieties, in many sizes and shapes, and the blocky fruit varieties, called sweet, bell or green pappers. While both are grown as annuals, they are hot-weather perennial shrubs. Their shiny foliage earns them consideration for space in flower gardens. Hot varieties become even hotter as they change color. Sweet pepper is often eaten green but its vitamin C content increases if it is left on vine to turn red. Grow a lot of these. Mellow loam. Too much nitrogen will result in beautiful plants but fewer peppers. Thirty-three plants in 50-foot row will produce 30 pounds of peppers.

PLANTING: Start plants indoors 8-10 weeks in advance of transplanting time, which is at least a week after the last spring frost. Start in flats or three-inch peat pots, with seeds half-inch deep. Set out plants 18 inches apart, in rows 30 inches apart, and slightly deeper than pot soil level. Water well and, if sunny and hot, shade after transplanting. Relatively quick-growing crops such as radishes or green onions can be planted in same row, and harvested before pepper plants reach their full growth.

CULTIVATION: Peppers develop at their own pace and gardener should not be worried if at times the plants seem to do nothing for long periods. After ground is warm, mulch heavily to keep down weeds and save moisture. Some recommend black plastic mulch. Plants may need irrigation in first few weeks after setting out, but usually not after that.

HARVESTING: Both sweet and hot are good to eat at all stages of growth. Cut peppers off plant with knife or scissors, half-inch from pepper cap. Sweet varieties excellent for freezing. Gardeners should let a few of these mature to redness, and decide which they prefer. Red or green, they are delicious in a variety of ways, cut up in tossed salads and as garnishes, or stuffed and baked. And surplus can be frozen or used in relishes. Hot peppers come in variety of shapes, sizes and colors, and are used fresh, cooked or pickled, and may be dried. At frost time, all peppers should be picked, or entire plants can be pulled and hung upside down in cool spot, making fruit available for several more weeks.

ENEMIES: Cutworms will level young plants. Place collars around tiny plants, and sift wood ashes around them. A friendly toad will dine on cutworms. Other troubles prevented if gardener keeps weeds out of the plants, doesn't plant them near bean plants, and avoids walking in them when plants are wet.

VARIETIES: *Vinedale* (60 days from transplanting into garden to fruit. Sweet variety. Small plants heavy with fruit). **California Wonder* (75 days. Sweet. Good for stuffing). *Stokes Early Hybrid* (60 days. Sweet. Each plant will produce 8-10 fruit). *Long Red Cayenne* (72 days. Hot. Easily dried). *Hungarian Wax* (65 days. Hot. Yellow changing to red. Six-inch fruit).

19 VARIETY	DATE PLANTED	AMOUNT PLANTED (ROW LENGTH)
1.		
2.		
3.		

HARVEST DATES VARIETY	EXPECTED	ACTUAL
1.		
2.		
3.		

SATISFIED WITH VARIETY, AMOUNT?

1.
2.
3.

NOTES

19 VARIETY	DATE PLANTED	AMOUNT PLANTED (ROW LENGTH)
1.		
2.		
3.		

HARVEST DATES VARIETY	EXPECTED	ACTUAL
1.		
2.		
3.		

SATISFIED WITH VARIETY, AMOUNT?

1.
2.
3.

NOTES

19 VARIETY	DATE PLANTED	AMOUNT PLANTED (ROW LENGTH)
1.		
2.		
3.		

HARVEST DATES VARIETY	EXPECTED	ACTUAL
1.		
2.		
3.		

SATISFIED WITH VARIETY, AMOUNT?

1.
2.
3.

NOTES

POTATO *(Solanum tuberosum)* Garden books often suggest home gardeners should not raise potatoes since they take a lot of room and, unlike corn, peas or tomatoes, aren't much better than store-bought potatoes. But the taste of small new potatoes, and the surprises in the fall of digging into each hill to see how many will be there, make potato-raising very satisfying. Try planting 10 pounds and judge for yourself. New varieties make it possible to grow this formerly northern crop as far south as Florida. Need mellow, fertile, acid, well-drained soil, not limed. Good to enrich soil with manure, dug in the previous fall. Five pounds in 50-foot row should produce more than 50 pounds.

PLANTING: Seed potatoes should be "greened" before planting by spreading them out for several weeks in warm but not sunny area, such as an enclosed porch. Cut them up several days before planting, to let them harden, and thus prevent rot. Cut seed potatoes into blocky chunks, each with at least two eyes. Planting time is week before last frost for early potatoes, month later for storage varieties. Two methods of planting suggested, and both can be tried the same season. One is to dig eight-inch trench in row, with rows 30 inches apart. Lay down two-inch layer of compost in trench. Place potato sections a foot apart, and cover with four inches of soil. As potatoes sprout and begin to grow, fill trench gradually, then mulch around plants. Second method is to place potato sections 10 inches apart in a row on the ground, then cover with foot-thick layer of hay mulch, keep it well watered and wait for crop.

CULTIVATION: Soak with water during dry spell. Keep well mulched, no matter which method of planting is used.

HARVESTING: After blossoms form, dig up a meal or two of the early variety when they are golf ball size or even smaller. A real delicacy. Dig as needed after that. Later crop, for storages, should be left in ground until fully mature, and harvest may be delayed as much as a month after first frost, unless weather is exceptionally warm or wet. Harvest can be started after most of tops have yellowed. Dig carefully, preferably when soil is dry. Dry potatoes for a few hours, then store them in dark room with high humidity and temperatures in 36-40 degree area.

ENEMIES: Potatoes are known to have as many as 60 diseases, but gardener should be assured that no crop yet has had all of those, and most can be avoided by following a few rules. Don't grow potatoes where tomatoes, eggplant or peppers have grown in the past three years. Don't put lime or fresh manure on soil before planting. Plant seed potato, certified as disease free, rather than those bought at grocery store. Mulch heavily. Colorado potato beetles may visit. Pick them off vines and, if not squeamish, pinch them, or otherwise destroy them. Also look for and pinch off any potato beetle eggs on underside of leaves. Use rotenone frequently. Plant beans nearby.

VARIETIES: Check your Extension Agent or some trustworthy gardener for varieties that grow well in your area. *Irish Cobbler* (80 Days to maturity. Early variety. High in vitamin C. Susceptible to most diseases). *Norland* (80 days. Early. Red-skinned. Resistant to common scab and rugose mosiac). *Kennebec* (110 days. Late maturing. Resistant to late blight and mosiacs. Susceptible to verticillium wilt). *Katahdin* (110 days. Late maturing. Good keeper).

19 VARIETY	DATE PLANTED	AMOUNT PLANTED (ROW LENGTH)
1.		
2.		
3.		

HARVEST DATES VARIETY	EXPECTED	ACTUAL
1.		
2.		
3.		

SATISFIED WITH VARIETY, AMOUNT?

1.
2.
3.

NOTES

19 VARIETY	DATE PLANTED	AMOUNT PLANTED (ROW LENGTH)
1.		
2.		
3.		

HARVEST DATES VARIETY	EXPECTED	ACTUAL
1.		
2.		
3.		

SATISFIED WITH VARIETY, AMOUNT?

1.
2.
3.

NOTES

19 VARIETY	DATE PLANTED	AMOUNT PLANTED (ROW LENGTH)
1.		
2.		
3.		

HARVEST DATES VARIETY	EXPECTED	ACTUAL
1.		
2.		
3.		

SATISFIED WITH VARIETY, AMOUNT?

1.
2.
3.

NOTES

PUMPKIN *(Cucurbita pepo)* This is a sprawling squash plant that is as intruding as a borrowing neighbor, but it must be raised if there are young members in the family. Scratch their names on their "own" young pumpkins and those names will appear large and plain at Halloween. As a space-saving maneuver, these can be interplanted with sweet corn, if you don't mind tripping over vines as you gather corn. Grown throughout United States. Stronger in flavor than squash, so less popular, but can be used in pies and bread. Likes rich, light soil. A quarter-ounce of seed in 50-foot row will yield at least 75 pounds.

PLANTING: Prepare hills five feet apart in each direction by digging in at least a spadeful of compost or well-rotted manure. Two weeks after last frost, plant two or three seeds one inch deep in each hill. When two inches high, cut all but strongest plant in each hill.

CULTIVATION: Mulch heavily, and insure ample moisture by irrigation if necessary. When all fruit that will mature by first frost have been set, pinch back vines, and remove fruits set too late to mature.

HARVESTING: Pumpkins must be harvested before Halloween or they will disappear. After first frost, cut them from vine with sharp knife, leaving three-inch handle. Allow to cure two or three weeks in field. Store them in cool, dry cellar.

ENEMIES: This is a hardy plant, well able to take care of itself if given a good start. Squash vine borner can be troublesome. If branch of vine wilts, cut into where wilt begins, look for him, and dig him out. In heat of day, check for squash bugs. Crush them, or douse them in kerosene. Look for their eggs, tiny brown clusters, and crush them also.

VARIETIES: *Big Max* (120 days. For the gardener who wants to make his reputation in pumpkins, this is the variety, since it will grow to 100 or more pounds. Start several vines, in individual hills that have been prepared with bushel or more of compost or well-rotted manure worked in. Let only one pumpkin start on each vine, and keep vines well watered, mulched and fed, and you'll win first prize at the county fair). **Small Sugar* (100 days. Best flavored. Weigh about seven pounds each. A good one to grow). **Cinderella* (95 days. Ten-inch pumpkins. The virtue of this variety is that its bush-like plant can be restrained into a six square foot area.).

19	VARIETY	DATE PLANTED	AMOUNT PLANTED (ROW LENGTH)
1.			
2.			
3.			

HARVEST DATES	VARIETY	EXPECTED	ACTUAL
1.			
2.			
3.			

SATISFIED WITH VARIETY, AMOUNT?		
1.		
2.		
3.		

NOTES ____________________

19	VARIETY	DATE PLANTED	AMOUNT PLANTED (ROW LENGTH)
1.			
2.			
3.			

HARVEST DATES	VARIETY	EXPECTED	ACTUAL
1.			
2.			
3.			

SATISFIED WITH VARIETY, AMOUNT?		
1.		
2.		
3.		

NOTES ____________________

19	VARIETY	DATE PLANTED	AMOUNT PLANTED (ROW LENGTH)
1.			
2.			
3.			

HARVEST DATES	VARIETY	EXPECTED	ACTUAL
1.			
2.			
3.			

SATISFIED WITH VARIETY, AMOUNT?		
1.		
2.		
3.		

NOTES ____________________

RADISH *(Raphanus sativus)* While radish-raising will never be as challenging to the gardener as the propagation of orchids, this spicy little root deserves a small place in everyone's garden as a lively harbinger of spring, enlivening the family salad and giving a tasty hint of the bounty the garden is about to offer. Cool weather vegetable, grown in winter in South, spring and fall in North. In most gardens in the North the radish is the first crop of spring to be eaten. Rich sandy loam. Half-ounce of seed in 50-foot row will yield 25 pounds. Frequently used to mark rows of slower-growing crops such as carrots and parsnips.

PLANTING: Dig layer of compost into row. As soon as soil can be worked, sow seed one inch apart in rows a foot apart. Cover with half-inch of sifted compost. Sow 10-foot sections of row every 10 days to insure an adequate continuing crop. Plant early varieties first, switch to summer varieties when weather warms up, then switch to late varieties.

CULTIVATION: For mild radishes, assure fast growth through early mulching and ample moisture.

HARVESTING: Pick early and summer varieties before or as they reach maturity. Leave late varieties in ground until after frost, then pull up and store in damp sand in cellar.

ENEMIES: To avoid maggots, avoid planting where any member of cabbage family has grown in past three years, and rake wood ashes into soil.

VARIETIES: *Cherry Belle* (22 days. Early. Round and smooth. Good eating). *Sparkler* (25 days. Round, red with lower portion of root white). *White Icicle* (28 days. Summer. Slender roots. White skin). *Celestial* (60 days. Late variety. 6-8 inch pure white root. Good to store).

19	VARIETY	DATE PLANTED	AMOUNT PLANTED (ROW LENGTH)
1.			
2.			
3.			

HARVEST DATES	VARIETY	EXPECTED	ACTUAL
1.			
2.			
3.			

SATISFIED WITH VARIETY, AMOUNT?

1. ____
2. ____
3. ____

NOTES ____

19	VARIETY	DATE PLANTED	AMOUNT PLANTED (ROW LENGTH)
1.			
2.			
3.			

HARVEST DATES	VARIETY	EXPECTED	ACTUAL
1.			
2.			
3.			

SATISFIED WITH VARIETY, AMOUNT?

1. ____
2. ____
3. ____

NOTES ____

19	VARIETY	DATE PLANTED	AMOUNT PLANTED (ROW LENGTH)
1.			
2.			
3.			

HARVEST DATES	VARIETY	EXPECTED	ACTUAL
1.			
2.			
3.			

SATISFIED WITH VARIETY, AMOUNT?

1. ____
2. ____
3. ____

NOTES ____

RHUBARB *(Rheum rhaponticum)* Hardy perennial grown for its tasty stalks. Leaves are poisonous. Can be grown throughout United States, but does not do well in Florida or on Gulf Coast, since it needs cold period of dormancy that comes when ground is frozen at least several inches deep. Sandy, slightly acid soil. Select site carefully for the half-dozen plants you will want, since this plant will grow for years in same location. Each mature plant will yield 6-8 pounds of stalk during the six-week spring season.

PLANTING: Prepare hills three feet apart by digging in quantity of leaf mold, rotted manure or compost. Crowns (also commonly called roots) should be set in soil deep enough so that top is four inches below surface. Firm soil around and over it. Planting can be in either spring or fall.

CULTIVATION: Mulch heavily. Oak leaves are good mulch. Feed each year with layer of compost, after harvesting spring crop, or in fall. If dry season, wet thoroughly, especially when large leaves are forming. Cut back flower stalks each summer as they develop, to conserve strength of plant. Each 4-5 years, when stalks become small, dig up and divide large clumps of roots, replanting them as described above (and offering a few to a rhubarbless neighbor).

HARVESTING: Don't for two years after planting. Third spring plants are in ground, harvest stalks with largest leaves, pulling and twisting stems from base, rather than cutting them. Leaves are good additions to compost pile. Do not strip plant. Take stalks at least one inch thick and 10 inches long. Leave short and thin stalks to feed roots for following year. After six weeks of intermittant harvesting, stop. Rhubard is good fresh in sauce or pies, is used in jelly, marmalade and relish, and freezes well. For a different treat try digging up a few roots after ground has frozen them, storing them in moist soil, letting them freeze outdoors, then, after at least six weeks, forcing them in winter by bring them into dark cellar where temperature is in the 50s. Keep humidity high and they will reward you with 2-6 pounds of delicately pink stems per root.

ENEMIES: Few enemies are strong enough to hamper the growth of this plant if it is kept fed and mulched.

VARIETIES: If starting crowns, proven in taste and hardiness for your area, cannot be obtained by barter or other means from a neighboring gardener, try one of following obtainable through commercial channels:

MacDonald (Grows well in most of country. Brilliant red stalks impart a pleasingly pink tone to sauces and pies. Does not have to be peeled). *Valentine* (Deep red, lengthy and thick stalks). *Cherry* (Grown in milder climates, such as on West Coast).

19	VARIETY	DATE PLANTED	AMOUNT PLANTED (ROW LENGTH)
1.			
2.			
3.			

HARVEST DATES	VARIETY	EXPECTED	ACTUAL
1.			
2.			
3.			

SATISFIED WITH VARIETY, AMOUNT?

1.
2.
3.

NOTES

19	VARIETY	DATE PLANTED	AMOUNT PLANTED (ROW LENGTH)
1.			
2.			
3.			

HARVEST DATES	VARIETY	EXPECTED	ACTUAL
1.			
2.			
3.			

SATISFIED WITH VARIETY, AMOUNT?

1.
2.
3.

NOTES

19	VARIETY	DATE PLANTED	AMOUNT PLANTED (ROW LENGTH)
1.			
2.			
3.			

HARVEST DATES	VARIETY	EXPECTED	ACTUAL
1.			
2.			
3.			

SATISFIED WITH VARIETY, AMOUNT?

1.
2.
3.

NOTES

RUTABAGA *(Brassica napobrassica)* Also called Swedish turnip, Swede turnip, winter turnip, yellow turnip. Not surprising, therefore, it is much like turnip in both cultivation and taste. Rutabagas do best in North, turnips South of Mason-Dixon Line. This hardy root crop is high in food value, easy to grow and stores well—better than turnip. However the enthusiastic gardener should make certain he has rutabaga-loving family or friends before sowing eighth of an ounce of seed in 50-foot row to yield 50 pounds of rutabagas. Moist, rich soil.

PLANTING: Must be planted in early summer to provide 90-100 days of growth by first fall frost. Sow seeds quarter-inch deep (barely cover with soil) as thin as possible in rows 18 inches apart. Thin to 8-12 inches apart, when plants are three inches high. Keep seedbed moist. Often is planted in row where early salad crops have been grown.

CULTIVATION: In heat of summer, provide young plants with plenty of moisture, and mulch well.

HARVESTING: About 90 days after planting, when roots are 4-5 inches across (much larger than turnips), grasp tops and pull them out. This can be after first frost, but should be done before ground is frozen, or keeping quality will be hampered. Can be stored in root cellar or pit or, buried in moist sand, in cellar. Some gardeners wax these, to prolong their storage life.

ENEMIES: All enemies of cabbage family should be guarded against, but seldom will they harm this hardy plant.

VARIETIES: There are both yellow and white varieties. *Burpee's Purple-Top Yellow* (90 days to harvest. Fine-grained yellow flesh. Good keeper). *Laurentian* (90 days. Deep purple top, smooth root, yellow flesh).

19	VARIETY	DATE PLANTED	AMOUNT PLANTED (ROW LENGTH)
1.			
2.			
3.			

HARVEST DATES	VARIETY	EXPECTED	ACTUAL
1.			
2.			
3.			

SATISFIED WITH VARIETY, AMOUNT?

1.
2.
3.

NOTES

19	VARIETY	DATE PLANTED	AMOUNT PLANTED (ROW LENGTH)
1.			
2.			
3.			

HARVEST DATES	VARIETY	EXPECTED	ACTUAL
1.			
2.			
3.			

SATISFIED WITH VARIETY, AMOUNT?

1.
2.
3.

NOTES

19	VARIETY	DATE PLANTED	AMOUNT PLANTED (ROW LENGTH)
1.			
2.			
3.			

HARVEST DATES	VARIETY	EXPECTED	ACTUAL
1.			
2.			
3.			

SATISFIED WITH VARIETY, AMOUNT?

1.
2.
3.

NOTES

SALSIFY *(Tragopogon porrifolius)* Also called oyster plant and vegetable oyster because of the taste of its roots when cooked. Every gardener should try this at least once. Good conversation crop since it is not widely grown and many gardeners have only heard about it. Growth is similar to parsnips, but growing season is longer. Light, mellow soil, well drained, with compost worked in deep. Avoid use of manure unless it is extremely well rotted. Plants grow 3-4 feet high, with tapering tap roots 8-10 inches in length, 1½ inches in diameter. In colder areas of North, gardeners dig 12-inch by 12-inch trench along row, fill it with compost, and plant seed in that, to get maximum growth. Half-ounce of seed in 50-foot row should produce more than 250 roots—far more than is needed for conversation.

PLANTING: Purchase fresh seed each year. Sow need half-inch deep, fairly thickly in rows 12-15 inches apart. When plants are three inches high, thin to stand 4 inches apart.

CULTIVATION: Mulch after thinning. Keep soil moist.

HARVESTING: Heavy frost improves flavor. Dig as needed after frost, or dig to store in root pit or root cellar, or in damp sand in cellar. May be left in ground and dug up in spring.

ENEMIES: If Salsify has few friends among gardeners, it has even fewer pest or disease enemies.

VARIETIES: *Sandwich Island Mammoth* (120 days. With creamy white root flesh) is only variety commonly available.

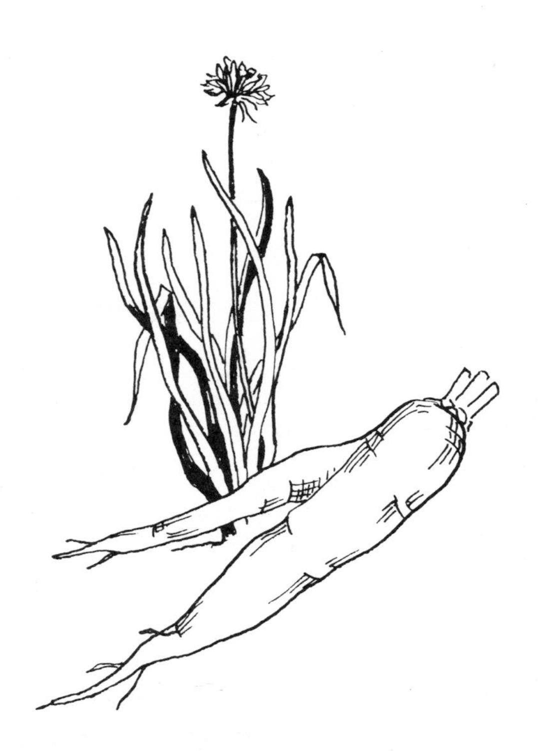

19	VARIETY	DATE PLANTED	AMOUNT PLANTED (ROW LENGTH)
1.			
2.			
3.			

HARVEST DATES	VARIETY	EXPECTED	ACTUAL
1.			
2.			
3.			

SATISFIED WITH VARIETY, AMOUNT?

1. ______
2. ______
3. ______

NOTES ______

19	VARIETY	DATE PLANTED	AMOUNT PLANTED (ROW LENGTH)
1.			
2.			
3.			

HARVEST DATES	VARIETY	EXPECTED	ACTUAL
1.			
2.			
3.			

SATISFIED WITH VARIETY, AMOUNT?

1. ______
2. ______
3. ______

NOTES ______

19	VARIETY	DATE PLANTED	AMOUNT PLANTED (ROW LENGTH)
1.			
2.			
3.			

HARVEST DATES	VARIETY	EXPECTED	ACTUAL
1.			
2.			
3.			

SATISFIED WITH VARIETY, AMOUNT?

1. ______
2. ______
3. ______

NOTES ______

SOYBEANS *(Glycine max)* These beans require a long season of 3-5 months of warm weather, so are not practical in northern United States. Used as shell beans, green or dried. Slower growing than other bush beans. Yield per unit of land is small so only those with large gardening areas should consider growing them. Five-six ounces of seed for 50-foot row will yield 15 pounds of pods, half of that amount in beans.

PLANTING: Dust seeds with nitrogen inoculant. Two weeks after last spring frost, plant seeds one inch deep, two inches apart in rows two (for early varieties) to three feet apart. Thin plants to 3-4 inches apart. Require fertile, well-drained, mellow soil with additional lime.

CULTIVATION: Shallow root system, so avoid deep cultivation. Mulch when plants are four inches tall.

HARVESTING: For use as green beans, harvest pods when beans are fully grown but before pods turn yellow. Harvest period is 7-10 days. Steam or parboil pods 4-5 minutes, in small batches, before attempting to shell them. To get dry soybeans, pick when beans are dry but stems are still green. Otherwise, if picking is delayed, pods will break, scattering beans. Dried beans are good for baking and sprouting.

ENEMIES: Soybeans are a favorite of rabbits. Diseases such as brown spot, bacterial blight and downy mildew can be avoided by rotating the crop with other crops, and composting the vines at the end of the season.

VARIETIES: **Kanrich* (103 days to harvest. Pods contain 2-3 beans. When green good as shell beans; when mature and dried, may be cooked similarly to lima beans).

19 VARIETY	DATE PLANTED	AMOUNT PLANTED (ROW LENGTH)
1.		
2.		
3.		

HARVEST DATES VARIETY	EXPECTED	ACTUAL
1.		
2.		
3.		

SATISFIED WITH VARIETY, AMOUNT?

1.
2.
3.

NOTES

19 VARIETY	DATE PLANTED	AMOUNT PLANTED (ROW LENGTH)
1.		
2.		
3.		

HARVEST DATES VARIETY	EXPECTED	ACTUAL
1.		
2.		
3.		

SATISFIED WITH VARIETY, AMOUNT?

1.
2.
3.

NOTES

19 VARIETY	DATE PLANTED	AMOUNT PLANTED (ROW LENGTH)
1.		
2.		
3.		

HARVEST DATES VARIETY	EXPECTED	ACTUAL
1.		
2.		
3.		

SATISFIED WITH VARIETY, AMOUNT?

1.
2.
3.

NOTES

SPINACH *(Spinacia oleracea)* Mothers' admonitions to their children to eat this vegetable have done much to diminish its popularity. Hardy, cool-weather plant grown in winter in South, in early spring and late fall in North. Will grow on any fertile soil, with plenty of nigrogen. Lime should be added if soil is at all acid. Half-ounce of seed in 50-foot row will produce 40 pounds of spinach.

PLANTING: Purchase fresh seed each year. As soon as ground can be worked, plant seed half-inch deep, one inch apart, in rows 12 inches apart. Thin seedlings to stand three inches apart. When spinach plants have grown enough to touch each other in row, harvest (and dine on) every other plant.

CULTIVATION: Mulch heavily after second thinning, avoiding use of any acid material such as oak leaves. Water every 3-4 days in dry season. Heat makes this plant bolt—blossom and form seeds. If this happens, spinach is ready to make its contribution to the compost pile.

HARVESTING: Patient gardener will cut outer leaves, allowing small center leaves to grow. The more common method, for those of us less virtuous, is to cut plants at root level. Good frozen. Pick a few of the first tender leaves for salad.

ENEMIES: Plant resistant varieties, keep well weeded or heavily mulched and remain ignorant of the diseases listed for this vegetable. Grow enough so that a loss in wet weather through damping-off will not leave children hungry. Hand pick the spinach flea beetle, a hungry quarter-inch greenish black fellow, and its larvae, both found on undersides of leaves.

VARIETIES: **Bloomsdale Long Standing* (48 days. Crinkle-leafed. Resists bolting). **Hybrid #7* (42 days. Resistant to downy mildew. Semi-savoyed leaves. Good for freezing and canning). *America* (50 days. Grows more slowly and remains edible longer. Slow to bolt).

19 VARIETY	DATE PLANTED	AMOUNT PLANTED (ROW LENGTH)
1.		
2.		
3.		

HARVEST DATES VARIETY	EXPECTED	ACTUAL
1.		
2.		
3.		

SATISFIED WITH VARIETY, AMOUNT?
1.
2.
3.

NOTES

19 VARIETY	DATE PLANTED	AMOUNT PLANTED (ROW LENGTH)
1.		
2.		
3.		

HARVEST DATES VARIETY	EXPECTED	ACTUAL
1.		
2.		
3.		

SATISFIED WITH VARIETY, AMOUNT?
1.
2.
3.

NOTES

19 VARIETY	DATE PLANTED	AMOUNT PLANTED (ROW LENGTH)
1.		
2.		
3.		

HARVEST DATES VARIETY	EXPECTED	ACTUAL
1.		
2.		
3.		

SATISFIED WITH VARIETY, AMOUNT?
1.
2.
3.

NOTES

SQUASH *(Cucurbita)* SUMMER. Prizes should be awarded gardeners who grow no more summer squash than they can use. This is one of the few garden crops that becomes difficult even to give away. Huge variety of these makes restraint in planting essential. A truly American plant, this grows throughout nation, and in abundance. A conservative estimate is that a quarter-ounce of seed in 50-foot row of hills will yield 150 squashes. Bush plants take far less space than vines.

PLANTING: Spade well-rotted manure or compost into sandy loam of each hill. Plant no more than 2-3 hills of each summer variety, saving greater part of space for winter varieties. Allow three feet between hills, four feet between rows. If vine types are selected, it is good to plant them at one side of garden, so vines can wander out into uncultivated areas. When danger of frost is past, soil is warm, plant three seeds per hill, half-inch deep and six inches apart. Seed is so viable it is not necessary to plant more and then thin.

HARVESTING: Pick early and often. Squash is best before it reaches maturity, and when can be indented easily with thumb nail. If squash unexpectedly grow too large—and they will if you so much as turn your back on them—pick them anyway and add them to compost pile. Not picking them will halt production of plants. Summer squash are best eaten fresh, but can be frozen with so-so results. Good raw, when young, in salad, or simply with mayonnaise. Also, raw slices can be used as a base for canapes, topped with various dips and spreads.

ENEMIES: If given a good start, these plants will nearly care for themselves. Use healthy seed, add compost to hills and rotate crop. The threat to summer squash is not nearly as formidable as this list of enemies might indicate. Squash bug, reddish-bown, dine on foliage. Can be trapped by laying shingles near plants, killing bugs under them early in morning. Plant nasturtiums or radishes or marigolds nearby to repel. Welcome the solemn toad to your garden. He will eat squash bugs, cutworms and many other undesirable visitors to your crops. Handpick squash bugs as well as their eggs, shiny brown, on underside of leaves.

The striped beetle has the appetite of an in-law and launches deadly attack against squash seedlings, appearing almost as if they were somehow planted with the squash seeds. If a serious problem, can be avoided by starting plants indoors. This can be difficult because of plant's taproot. Beetles can be hand picked. For definite control, form tent of cheesecloth over plant, tucking edges under soil. Or make boxes 18 inches square, 10 inches high, without top or bottom. Set over hill, banking earth around it. Cover top with cheesecloth.

Squash borer: Easily spotted. He's usually guilty if mature vine suddenly wilts. Using sharp knife, slit vine back to where white grub, the borer, will be found. Do him in, then cover slit stem with soil, giving it a chance to form roots. Defense against the borer can be set up by covering short sections of vine with soil in advance.

VARIETIES: There are more good ones than can be listed, so read seed catalogs and experiment widely—but with number of hills held well in check.
Early Prolific Straightneck (50 days. Bush. Good for all uses. Creamy yellow fruit good from 4-6 inch growth until they are 12-14 inches long). *White Bush Patty Pan* (54 days. Bush. Deliciously mild). *Zucchini* (50 days. Bush. Good flavor and prolific. Grow a few so you will have them for those many zucchini recipes that are published each summer).

19 VARIETY	DATE PLANTED	AMOUNT PLANTED (ROW LENGTH)
1.		
2.		
3.		

HARVEST DATES VARIETY	EXPECTED	ACTUAL
1.		
2.		
3.		

SATISFIED WITH VARIETY, AMOUNT?

1. ___
2. ___
3. ___

NOTES ___

19 VARIETY	DATE PLANTED	AMOUNT PLANTED (ROW LENGTH)
1.		
2.		
3.		

HARVEST DATES VARIETY	EXPECTED	ACTUAL
1.		
2.		
3.		

SATISFIED WITH VARIETY, AMOUNT?

1. ___
2. ___
3. ___

NOTES ___

19 VARIETY	DATE PLANTED	AMOUNT PLANTED (ROW LENGTH)
1.		
2.		
3.		

HARVEST DATES VARIETY	EXPECTED	ACTUAL
1.		
2.		
3.		

SATISFIED WITH VARIETY, AMOUNT?

1. ___
2. ___
3. ___

NOTES ___

SQUASH, *(Cucurbita)* WINTER. Select several varieties and be prepared to sacrifice a lot of garden space for the delicious squash you will raise. Grown throughout the United States, with each area having its favorites. Plant squash in sandy loam, adding several shovelsful of compost to each hill location. Half-ounce of seed in hills in 50-foot row will yield 75 or more pounds of squash, depending on variety.

PLANTING: If garden is adjacent to uncultivated area, plant squash there so vines can rampage out of garden, rather than across rows of carefully cultivated plants. Set hills at least 5-6 feet apart. After all danger of frost is past, set seeds inch-deep in soil, two to hill. Can be started indoors month in advance, but care must be taken in transplanting, due to lengthy tap root that will be developed.

CULTIVATION: Mulch heavily before vines begin their extensive wandering. Keep soil moist. When vines are lengthy, put section of vine in contact with soil, and cover it with soil, so that it will form roots, and lessen danger of squash borers. For large squash, such as Hubbards, top dress with compost, pinch back vines and leave no more than two fruits on each vine. With bush squash, mulch tightly around them.

HARVESTING: Unlike summer squash, winter type must mature fully on the vines, attaining full growth and hardened skins, for best storage characteristics. Cut squash off vine with sharp knife before first frost, handle gently, let cure in sun, wash and wipe carefully, then store all sound fruit in dry cellar, with temperatures between 40° and 50°. To avoid a rotting mold, wipe squash with oily cloth.

ENEMIES: Like summer squash, the winter varieties are hardy if given a good start. Striped beetle is greatest threat to the seedlings, and will devour them if not hand-picked or otherwise discouraged. Cheesecloth tents, held over plants with stakes and with edges tucked into soil, will foil this intruder.

Try planting a few nasturtiums, radishes or marigolds in or near each hill to repel the squash bug. If this intruder, in the egg, nymph or adult stage, is found, he should be hand picked. Look on underside of leaves for them. A wilted vine is the calling card of the squash borer, and he can be tracked down and destroyed by judicious use of sharp knife, slicing lengthwise into stem near point where wilting begins. A white grubby type, he should be taken out and killed, and the cut section of vine covered with soil, giving it an opportunity to root itself.

VARIETIES: Experiment with several, to find the ones you like the best. Try these: *Butternut* (85 days. Tops on the list for flavor. Good keeper and resistant to the squash borer). **Blue Hubbard* (120 days. A traditional variety, with impressive 15-pounders not at all uncommon. Good keeper and tasty. To break through their armor-like interior to get at the eating within, drop them on a concrete floor). *Gold Nugget* (85 days. Bush type. Requires little room. Buttercup-shaped, bright orange fruit with deep yellow flesh. Good baked in shell). *Table Queen* or *Acorn* (80 days. Good baked in shell, with half making a serving. A favorite of most housewives).

19	VARIETY	DATE PLANTED	AMOUNT PLANTED (ROW LENGTH)
1.			
2.			
3.			

HARVEST DATES	VARIETY	EXPECTED	ACTUAL
1.			
2.			
3.			

SATISFIED WITH VARIETY, AMOUNT?

1.
2.
3.

NOTES

19	VARIETY	DATE PLANTED	AMOUNT PLANTED (ROW LENGTH)
1.			
2.			
3.			

HARVEST DATES	VARIETY	EXPECTED	ACTUAL
1.			
2.			
3.			

SATISFIED WITH VARIETY, AMOUNT?

1.
2.
3.

NOTES

19	VARIETY	DATE PLANTED	AMOUNT PLANTED (ROW LENGTH)
1.			
2.			
3.			

HARVEST DATES	VARIETY	EXPECTED	ACTUAL
1.			
2.			
3.			

SATISFIED WITH VARIETY, AMOUNT?

1.
2.
3.

NOTES

STRAWBERRY *(Fragaria)* Grown throughout United States, and a favorite everywhere. Even a small bed is valuable in the kitchen garden. Superior in flavor to commercial varieties. They are more work than most other crops. Select site carefully and early. It should have rich loam, have been cultivated for at least two years, and is ideal if it slopes slightly to the south so that water will not settle on it and it warms up early in the spring. To build up its humus content, barnyard manure (as much as 500 pounds to each 1,000 square feet) should be worked into it in the fall, with a layer of compost added in the spring. Unless the soil is extremely acid (below pH 5.0), don't add lime. Fifty-foot row should produce 30 quarts in season, with this yield varying according to variety planted, method used in setting out plants, and fertility of soil.

PLANTING: Order plants early, to get varieties wanted. Plants should be certified to be disease and virus-free. They may be set out as soon as ground can be worked. In South, this can be done in fall. The many systems of placing plants should be studied. A favorite for home gardeners is to buy one plant per yard of row (thus 33 plants for 100-foot row). Set plants three feet apart in row, and let two runners set, in row and on either side of plant. After first full harvest (one year plus that spring's harvest), dig out original plants, and let runners from those remaining replace them. Three such rows can be set a foot apart, with two-foot space between each three rows. Such a plan produces a self-perpetuating bed. Water new plants well when setting them out, and shade for a few days if necessary.

CULTIVATION: Careful, heavy mulching will prevent troublesome weed problems. Runners you want to establish will push roots down through mulch. Remove all buds and unwanted runners the first year. Beginning gardeners are tempted to let more runners root, believing this will increase yield. It will only result in crowded, unhealthy plants and small berries. After first heavy freeze, mulch over entire bed with hay, straw or pine boughs. This should be removed gradually early each spring, leaving enough to cover ground. Compost should be spread in rows at end of each harvest.

HARVESTING: No berries should be allowed to mature first year. Keep ripened berries picked. Good time to pick a few is first thing in the morning, to top a bowl of cereal.

ENEMIES: Proper selection and preparation of bed site, and purchase of certified plants will discourage most of these. Place shingles near fruit clusters. Look under them in morning. If slugs are found, surprise them with a sprinkle of salt, and they will disappear. Fungus diseases are greater threat, particularly in wet weather. Leaf spot (small reddish-brown spots on leaves with spots becoming white in the center) is prevalent wherever strawberries are grown, particularly in cool, wet weather. Leaf scorch looks much the same on the leaves, but lacks the white centered spot. Both will reduce yield or at worst kill plants. After harvest mow all leaves off plants and burn them. If either persists, start new bed as far as possible from old bed, with virus-resistant stock.

VARIETIES: Find out which varieties do well in your area. These are good: **Fairfax* (Early fruiting. Resistant to leaf spot, leaf scorch and red stele. Flavorful and a good freezer). *Catskill* (Midseason. Beautiful and large, but susceptible to leaf spot and leaf scorch). **Sparkle* (late fruiting. Susceptible to leaf spot and leaf scorch. Good flavor and color. Freezes well). The beginner will read about *Everbearing Strawberries* and be entranced by the promise of spring, summer and fall berries. They aren't recommended, since the yield is so light.

19 VARIETY	DATE PLANTED	AMOUNT PLANTED (ROW LENGTH)
1.		
2.		
3.		

HARVEST DATES VARIETY	EXPECTED	ACTUAL
1.		
2.		
3.		

SATISFIED WITH VARIETY, AMOUNT?

1.
2.
3.

NOTES

19 VARIETY	DATE PLANTED	AMOUNT PLANTED (ROW LENGTH)
1.		
2.		
3.		

HARVEST DATES VARIETY	EXPECTED	ACTUAL
1.		
2.		
3.		

SATISFIED WITH VARIETY, AMOUNT?

1.
2.
3.

NOTES

19 VARIETY	DATE PLANTED	AMOUNT PLANTED (ROW LENGTH)
1.		
2.		
3.		

HARVEST DATES VARIETY	EXPECTED	ACTUAL
1.		
2.		
3.		

SATISFIED WITH VARIETY, AMOUNT?

1.
2.
3.

NOTES

SUNFLOWER *(Helianthus annuus)* For an impressive display of green thumbery, grow a few dozen of these giants near those Big Max pumpkins. Sunflowers are ornamental, good for screening, and seeds are valued by both man and bird. Home gardeners raise the big variety, but smaller varieties have been developed for farm crops, and can be harvested easily with farm machinery. Need fertile soil, deeply prepared, with a large quantity of humus. Heavy feeders. Packet of seeds more than enough for 50-foot row yielding 25 enormous heads.

SOWING: Two weeks before last frost date, plant seeds in north end of garden or in bed exclusively for them, so they will not shade other crops. Space seeds foot apart, and plant one inch deep. For best crop, thin to 24 inches apart.

CULTIVATION: Mulch and provide adequate moisture. The gigantic sunflowers will require strong support, and high up near bloom, when seeds begin to fill out. This can be a sturdy pole for each plant, or a high fence (and the usual four-foot fence is not high enough) to which each plant can be loosely tied.

HARVESTING: The gathering of appreciative birds will signal harvesting time. The back of the heads will be turning brown, and they will droop to the ground unless supported. Cut heads with two feet of stem and hang to dry in warm, well-ventilated place, such as an attic. They can also be spread in the sun, guarded from birds, to dry. When heads are dry, seeds can be extracted with stiff brush. If seeds are still damp, spread to dry before storing.

ENEMIES: Stem borer, a grub, digs into stem and will kill plant. Cut into stem, slitting up and down it with knife, until borer is found.

VARIETIES: *Mammoth Russian* (80 days. This is the one to grow for big results. Grow 12 or more feet in height, with heads 15-20 inches in diameter. Seeds are rich and tasty). *Manchurian* (83 days. Tall stems, large seeds. Good yields).

19	VARIETY	DATE PLANTED	AMOUNT PLANTED (ROW LENGTH)
1.			
2.			
3.			

HARVEST DATES	VARIETY	EXPECTED	ACTUAL
1.			
2.			
3.			

SATISFIED WITH VARIETY, AMOUNT?

1. ______
2. ______
3. ______

NOTES ______

19	VARIETY	DATE PLANTED	AMOUNT PLANTED (ROW LENGTH)
1.			
2.			
3.			

HARVEST DATES	VARIETY	EXPECTED	ACTUAL
1.			
2.			
3.			

SATISFIED WITH VARIETY, AMOUNT?

1. ______
2. ______
3. ______

NOTES ______

19	VARIETY	DATE PLANTED	AMOUNT PLANTED (ROW LENGTH)
1.			
2.			
3.			

HARVEST DATES	VARIETY	EXPECTED	ACTUAL
1.			
2.			
3.			

SATISFIED WITH VARIETY, AMOUNT?

1. ______
2. ______
3. ______

NOTES ______

SWEET POTATO *(Ipomoea batatas)* Trailing vine cultivated for its luscious roots. A Southern crop, but are grown as far north as southern New York and southern Michigan. Need light sandy soil that is well-drained and a growing season of 150 warm days with night temperatures of 60° and preferably higher. Fifty slips planted in 50-foot row yields 50 pounds.

PLANTING: Except in deep South, sweet potatoes are started indoors, to stretch season enough for a good crop. They are started from slips, purchased or grown by gardener. To start slips, begin a month before night temperatures will remain above 60°. In hotbed, lay sweet potatoes on their sides and cover with two inches of moist sand. Get temperature up to 75-80°. Sprout slips 6-9 inches long will develop. These may be broken off with a twisting tug. In garden, in each row, form a foot-wide ridge 8-10 inches high, used for planting so roots will not be too deep for harvesting. Set slips a foot apart on top of ridge, and press four inches of each slip into ground. Water to settle slip. Space rows 3½ feet apart.

CULTIVATION: Keep weed-free until thick vines take over this job. Then mulch. Water well until vines begin to spread. After that the roots will be deep enough to find the moisture the plants require. Lift and move vines every few weeks to prevent them from rooting at the vine joints.

HARVESTING: Dig them before first frost, and preferably when soil is fairly dry. Use spading fork carefully, to avoid bruising them. Eat damaged potatoes first. Let those harvested dry 2-3 hours in field, then cure them for 10 days in 85° temperature. Then gradually reduce temperature to 50-55°.

VARIETIES: Ask gardeners in area which varieties grow best there. *Centennial* (150 days. Moist variety. Good yield). *Jersey Orange* (150 days. Dry-fleshed variety).

19	VARIETY	DATE PLANTED	AMOUNT PLANTED (ROW LENGTH)
1.			
2.			
3.			

HARVEST DATES	VARIETY	EXPECTED	ACTUAL
1.			
2.			
3.			

SATISFIED WITH VARIETY, AMOUNT?

1.
2.
3.

NOTES

19	VARIETY	DATE PLANTED	AMOUNT PLANTED (ROW LENGTH)
1.			
2.			
3.			

HARVEST DATES	VARIETY	EXPECTED	ACTUAL
1.			
2.			
3.			

SATISFIED WITH VARIETY, AMOUNT?

1.
2.
3.

NOTES

19	VARIETY	DATE PLANTED	AMOUNT PLANTED (ROW LENGTH)
1.			
2.			
3.			

HARVEST DATES	VARIETY	EXPECTED	ACTUAL
1.			
2.			
3.			

SATISFIED WITH VARIETY, AMOUNT?

1.
2.
3.

NOTES

SWISS CHARD *(Beta vulgaris cicla)* A beet grown for its tops, as greens. Valuable in garden as they send down long, powerful roots that will break up heavy subsoil. Grown throughout United States. Rich, mellow soil, not acid, should be enriched with layer of compost. Only a single planting is required. Quarter-ounce of seed sparsely sowed in 50-foot row will yield 50 pounds of chard.

PLANTING: Soak seed 24 hours before planting. As soon as ground can be prepared plant seeds 3-4 inches apart, in rows 18 inches apart. Cover with an inch of finely sifted compost.

CULTIVATION: Keep heavily mulched and moist.

HARVESTING: When plants are six inches tall, thin by removing (and using in salads or as greens) every other plant. When plants are seven inches tall, begin harvesting by cutting outer leaves with sharp knife. Harvest can continue throughout season if inside small leaves are permitted to grow. In mild climates, mulched plants will produce greens throughout winter. If roots are thus kept alive, a spring crop of greens can be anticipated. Greens are cooked like spinach.

ENEMIES: Mexican bean beetles can be hand picked (along with their yellow caterpillar larvae) and their eggs on underside of leaves should be crushed. Interplant with marigolds and nasturtiums. If rabbits begin sampling, spoil their dinner by dusting with a mixture of a box of cayenne pepper to three cups of flour.

VARIETIES: **Fordhook Giant* (60 days to first cutting. Heavily crumpled leaves). **Ruby* (60 days. A bright crimson rhubarb chard, with sweet flavor).

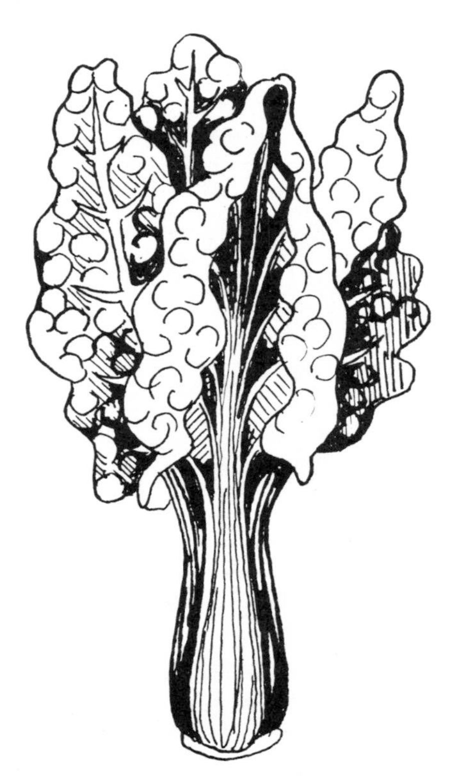

19	VARIETY	DATE PLANTED	AMOUNT PLANTED (ROW LENGTH)
1.			
2.			
3.			

HARVEST DATES	VARIETY	EXPECTED	ACTUAL
1.			
2.			
3.			

SATISFIED WITH VARIETY, AMOUNT?

1.
2.
3.

NOTES

19	VARIETY	DATE PLANTED	AMOUNT PLANTED (ROW LENGTH)
1.			
2.			
3.			

HARVEST DATES	VARIETY	EXPECTED	ACTUAL
1.			
2.			
3.			

SATISFIED WITH VARIETY, AMOUNT?

1.
2.
3.

NOTES

19	VARIETY	DATE PLANTED	AMOUNT PLANTED (ROW LENGTH)
1.			
2.			
3.			

HARVEST DATES	VARIETY	EXPECTED	ACTUAL
1.			
2.			
3.			

SATISFIED WITH VARIETY, AMOUNT?

1.
2.
3.

NOTES

TOMATOES *(Lycopersicon esculentum)* A must crop in every home garden, with the picking of the first tomatoes something of a holiday. Because of so many varieties, gardener should experiment with several each year until he discovers those that serve him best. Few gardeners will agree on that selection, or how to start, space and support them, and it is to the credit of the plant that it will produce well when subjected to the oddest of these ideas. Because of the hundreds of uses of tomatoes, plant more than enough. Tomatoes grow throughout the United States, in the winter in the extreme South, and in the spring, summer and fall further north. Fifty-foot row of 12-15 plants will yield minimum of 100 pounds of tomatoes.

PLANTING: In North start plants indoors, 6-8 weeks before time to transplant to garden, which is after last spring frost. May be started in flats (seeds one inch apart and quarter-inch deep), then, when true leaves form, transplanted to three-inch peat pots. These pots should be kept in moderate temperatures, with plenty of ventilation, to get stocky plants for garden. Nothing except headaches and worries gained by setting plants outdoors too soon. When danger of frost is past, enrich hills with compost, then set plants deep (a tomato plant will grow if only its tip is left above ground, although this is not recommended), three feet apart in rows four feet apart. Wet well to set soil around them. At same time set a five-foot stake beside each plant, so roots will not be disturbed by pounding a post through the roots later. Plants can be left to sprawl on ground if you want to share a larger crop with slugs, lose tomatoes under foliage.

CULTIVATION: In northern areas, mulch heavily only when soil is warm—about time plants blossom. Until then, cultivate to keep weeds down, and provide moisture if needed. For those who wisely stake their tomatoes, plants should be supported with the tie, and the knot tied tightly around post, not around stem. Sheets torn into ½ inch strips make good material for tying. The suckers that pop out between the branches and main stem of the tomato plant should be removed. This is a good job when gardener wants to enjoy garden without really working hard in it.

HARVESTING: Let tomatoes ripen on vine for best eating. Keep them picked. When frost threatens, pull plants, hang them upside down in cool place. Or pick green tomatoes, place them in cold frame on hay. Or wrap each in newspaper, place them in boxes with not more than two layers per box, and they will gradually ripen.

ENEMIES: If cutworms are a problem, place paper collars around plants, with collar extending at least an inch above and below the soil level. Search out and destroy the tomato worm. This worm is huge, green and has an appetite for foliage to match his size. Rotenone will halt the flea beetle from eating tiny holes in leaves.

Many diseases can be avoided by planting resistant seeds, giving plants ample room, providing plenty of humus and moisture, and not working in them when plants are wet.

VARIETIES: This is only a sample. The choice is wide, and should be tried. *Pixie Hybrid* (52 days after transplanting to harvest. For the gardener who wants the first tomato in his neighborhood. It is small but has a true "tomato" taste. Will grow indoors or out). *Fireball* (60 days. Early. Compact plants. Large crop of small to medium fruit). *Marglobe* (73 days. High yield and large, sweet fruit). *Big Boy* (78 days. This hybrid is a satisfying tomato, good taste and large enough so that one thick slice is big enough for a tomato sandwich—with tomato showing around the sides). *Burpee's VF Hybrid* (72 days. A good main crop tomato, offering meaty, tasty fruit in good quantity, and disease-resistant plants).

19	VARIETY	DATE PLANTED	AMOUNT PLANTED (ROW LENGTH)
1.			
2.			
3.			

HARVEST DATES	VARIETY	EXPECTED	ACTUAL
1.			
2.			
3.			

SATISFIED WITH VARIETY, AMOUNT?

1.
2.
3.

NOTES

19	VARIETY	DATE PLANTED	AMOUNT PLANTED (ROW LENGTH)
1.			
2.			
3.			

HARVEST DATES	VARIETY	EXPECTED	ACTUAL
1.			
2.			
3.			

SATISFIED WITH VARIETY, AMOUNT?

1.
2.
3.

NOTES

19	VARIETY	DATE PLANTED	AMOUNT PLANTED (ROW LENGTH)
1.			
2.			
3.			

HARVEST DATES	VARIETY	EXPECTED	ACTUAL
1.			
2.			
3.			

SATISFIED WITH VARIETY, AMOUNT?

1.
2.
3.

NOTES

TURNIP *(Brassica rapa)* This cool-season vegetable is raised for both its roots and tops. The latter can be eaten as greens. While turnips can be grown throughout the United States, they do best in the South, where they are raised to be harvested in winter and spring. In North, they are often planted in midsummer to be harvested after first frost, but can be planted in early spring. Moist, rich soil, but not too heavy with nitrogen. A quarter-ounce of seed in a 50-foot row will yield 50 pounds.

PLANTING: For early crop, sow as soon as ground can be worked. For later crop, in North, sow two months before first killing frost. Can be planted to follow spinach, peas or lettuce. Sow seed ½-inch deep, very sparsely, cover with sifted compost, in rows 18 inches apart. Moisten with gentle spray.

CULTIVATION: When about three inches high thin to 3-4 inches apart and use thinnings for greens. Make certain rows have enough moisture at first, before the deep root system is developed. Mulch heavily.

HARVESTING: Early crop may be harvested when roots are two inches in diameter. Harvest fall crop after first frosts, cut off tops and store in root cellar, where it is cool and damp. Odor may become objectionable if stored in cellar. Doesn't store as well as rutabaga.

ENEMIES: If cabbage worms sample your turnips, dust them with rotenone. Interplant with sage or rosemary.

VARIETIES: *Purple-top White Globe* (55 days. So crisp and tasty it can be eaten raw. Harvest when 2-3 inches in diameter). *Purple-top Milan* (45 days. Try this for an early crop). *Shogoin* (30 days to greens, 70 days for roots. Delicious).

19	VARIETY	DATE PLANTED	AMOUNT PLANTED (ROW LENGTH)
1.			
2.			
3.			

HARVEST DATES	VARIETY	EXPECTED	ACTUAL
1.			
2.			
3.			

SATISFIED WITH VARIETY, AMOUNT?

1.
2.
3.

NOTES

19	VARIETY	DATE PLANTED	AMOUNT PLANTED (ROW LENGTH)
1.			
2.			
3.			

HARVEST DATES	VARIETY	EXPECTED	ACTUAL
1.			
2.			
3.			

SATISFIED WITH VARIETY, AMOUNT?

1.
2.
3.

NOTES

19	VARIETY	DATE PLANTED	AMOUNT PLANTED (ROW LENGTH)
1.			
2.			
3.			

HARVEST DATES	VARIETY	EXPECTED	ACTUAL
1.			
2.			
3.			

SATISFIED WITH VARIETY, AMOUNT?

1.
2.
3.

NOTES

WATERMELON *(Citrullus vulgaris)* While originally a tropical African plant, watermelon can now be grown in much of the United States, due to quicker maturing varieties that have been developed, and by starting them in greenhouses. Gardeners everywhere should note it takes some 36 square feet to produce four watermelons, and decide whether such use of space is worthwhile. Sandy, slightly acid soil with a lot of humus needed. This plant wants moisture at all times. Packet of seeds in eight hills for 50-foot row will produce 25-30 watermelons.

PLANTING: For a good crop, a minimum of four months of frost-free weather is essential. Plant when all danger of frost is past. To lengthen growing season enough to get yield in North, start plants indoors, 6-8 weeks in advance of garden-planting time. Place three seeds half-inch deep in soil in three-inch peat pots. Thin to one per pot by clipping off all but the strongest vine when the growth has reached 12 inches. In North, after danger of frost is past, plant three pots a foot apart in each hill. If planting seeds, place 6-8 seeds half-inch deep and 2-3 inches apart. Hills, with both pots and seeds, should be 6-8 feet apart each way.

CULTIVATION: Hoe discreetly for several weeks to keep weeds down. Then, when ground is warm, mulch heavily. Do this before fruits form, to avoid moving vines at that time. To speed development of fruit, many growers limit to two the number of watermelon per vine. Late-set fruit should be removed.

HARVESTING: Fruits must ripen on the vine. Judging when they should be picked requires practice. Lighter area of melon should turn to creamy white. Plug can be taken. Experts judge by sound made when knuckles are rapped on melon.

ENEMIES: Avoid many of them by crop rotation, planting resistant varieties only once every five years in same place. Cucumber beetles will attack vines. Try interplanting with nasturtiums, radishes or marigolds. Hot caps can be used to protect young vines.

VARIETIES: *New Hampshire Midget* (70 days. The one to try in the North when you've been told you can't grow watermelon in your garden. 5-6 inch fruit with thin rind and good flavor). *Sugar Baby* (75 days. Larger than N.H. Midget. Sweet variety). *Dixie Queen* (90 days. Wilt resistant. Crisp, sweet flesh).

19	VARIETY	DATE PLANTED	AMOUNT PLANTED (ROW LENGTH)
1.			
2.			
3.			

HARVEST DATES	VARIETY	EXPECTED	ACTUAL
1.			
2.			
3.			

SATISFIED WITH VARIETY, AMOUNT?

1.
2.
3.

NOTES

19	VARIETY	DATE PLANTED	AMOUNT PLANTED (ROW LENGTH)
1.			
2.			
3.			

HARVEST DATES	VARIETY	EXPECTED	ACTUAL
1.			
2.			
3.			

SATISFIED WITH VARIETY, AMOUNT?

1.
2.
3.

NOTES

19	VARIETY	DATE PLANTED	AMOUNT PLANTED (ROW LENGTH)
1.			
2.			
3.			

HARVEST DATES	VARIETY	EXPECTED	ACTUAL
1.			
2.			
3.			

SATISFIED WITH VARIETY, AMOUNT?

1.
2.
3.

NOTES

VEGETABLE:

PLANTING:

HARVESTING:

ENEMIES:

VARIETIES:

19	VARIETY	DATE PLANTED	AMOUNT PLANTED (ROW LENGTH)
1.			
2.			
3.			

HARVEST DATES	VARIETY	EXPECTED	ACTUAL
1.			
2.			
3.			

SATISFIED WITH VARIETY, AMOUNT?

1. ______
2. ______
3. ______

NOTES ______

19	VARIETY	DATE PLANTED	AMOUNT PLANTED (ROW LENGTH)
1.			
2.			
3.			

HARVEST DATES	VARIETY	EXPECTED	ACTUAL
1.			
2.			
3.			

SATISFIED WITH VARIETY, AMOUNT?

1. ______
2. ______
3. ______

NOTES ______

19	VARIETY	DATE PLANTED	AMOUNT PLANTED (ROW LENGTH)
1.			
2.			
3.			

HARVEST DATES	VARIETY	EXPECTED	ACTUAL
1.			
2.			
3.			

SATISFIED WITH VARIETY, AMOUNT?

1. ______
2. ______
3. ______

NOTES ______

INDEX